12   46   £3.99

C000213046

Modern Wildfowling

MODERN WILDFOWLING

by

Eric Begbie

SWAN HILL
PRESS

DEDICATION

This book is dedicated to
the sons of solitude, the lonely ones.

THE WILDFOWLER

'The true philosopher of the gun is the wildfowler, for he must have the sensitive eye of an artist, a love of solitude and lonely places. He measures beauty by the flash of a bird's wing, by the glint of dawn on sliding waters, by the march of slow clouds. He is the son of solitude, the lonely one.'

J. Wentworth Day
Wild Wings

Copyright © Eric Begbie, 1990

British Library Cataloguing in Publication Data
Begbie, Eric
Modern wildfowling
New ed.
1. Great Britain. Wildfowling
I.   Title
799.2440941

ISBN 1 85310 155 9

First edition published in the UK 1980 by Saiga Publishing Co. Ltd.

This edition first published in the UK 1990 by Swan Hill Press,
an imprint of Airlife Publishing Ltd.

Printed in England by Livesey Ltd., Shrewsbury.

Swan Hill Press
An Imprint of Airlife Publishing
101 Longden Road, Shrewsbury SY3 9EB, England.

Contents

Acknowledgements

I would like to acknowledge with grateful thanks the assistance given by the undernoted individuals and organisations:

Bernard Barker, who painted the colour illustrations and drew the identification silhouettes. Without his help, the problems of identifying wildfowl in field conditions would have been much less easily dealt with; Jim Humphreys of Little Chart, Kent, for permission to reproduce his fine Italian print on page 18; the Blandford Press for their consent to quoting from *Wild Wings* by James Wentworth Day on the dedication page; the staff of BASC for much advice and information over many years; my wildfowling friends and acquaintances throughout Britain for their invaluable support, advice and guidance; and last, but not least, my wife and family for their tolerance and patience during the months that I paid more attention to my word processor than to them.

FEN BIRD SHOOTING.

Introduction

Driving along the south shore of Loch Leven on a balmy Sunday evening in September I drew into the side of the road to watch the long boats of the trout anglers heading back towards the pier at Kinross. The orange cast of the autumn sky was reflected in the calm waters of the loch and I was marvelling at the picture before me when a slight movement along the edge of a rose-tinted cloud caught my eye. With a discernible quickening of my pulse, I reached for the binoculars which lay, as always, in the parcel shelf of the Land Rover.

There could be no mistaking the identity of the birds which headed towards the loch at an incredible height. Minutes later, as they literally tumbled out of the sky to wiffle down upon the greensward of St Serf's Island, I confirmed from the calendar indicator of my wristwatch that it was the sixteenth of the month. They were a day early.

Every year, on or around 17 September, the first battalions of pinkfooted geese arrive in Scotland from their breeding grounds in the central oasis of Iceland. Leaving their summer retreat to the ravages of approaching winter, they make an amazing non-stop journey of over 800 miles to drop in on Loch Leven and a few other selected sites.

During the weeks which follow, their numbers build up and then, towards the beginning of October, they are joined by their larger cousins, the greylag. In other parts of Britain similar — and sometimes longer — migrations are ending as the barnacle geese arrive on Islay and the Solway, whitefronts fly in to Slimbridge and the rapidly increasing flocks of brent geese make their landfall in south-east England.

For many, many years the annual movements of the great birds have given man cause to wonder. In Britain we are more fortunate than most in the number and variety of geese which winter on our shores and inland waters.

Each year my shooting season commences with grouse in August and a few early mallard may grace the bag in September. The pleasures of moor and pond pale into insignificance, however, when compared to the wild anticipation which floods the mind when straining ears pick up the first musical sounds of incoming pinkfeet. There is a magic exuded by the great skeins which cannot be matched elsewhere in the world of nature.

Wildfowling is the pursuit of wild fowl in wild places. Wildfowling is a ragged skein of greylag battling against a howling gale in a December dawn as dark storm clouds scud across a slowly lightening sky. Wildfowling is the evocative whistle of wigeon, barely visible under a waning moon.

Technically the sport has been defined as the shooting of geese, duck and waders with a smoothbore shotgun. Such description does, I fear, allow the inclusion of such non-wildfowling activities as decoying semi-tame mallard on a well-fed flight pond or shooting hungry geese as they drop on to a potato field or barley stubble. Without wishing to denigrate any man's favoured sport, I must suggest that to detach the 'wild' from 'fowling' is to destroy the very nature of the art and, in consequence, this book does not dwell for long upon the gentleman's diversions of duck-shooting or goose-shooting. It is concerned with mud and storms and danger and wildfowl. Especially wildfowl.

Because the sport of wildfowling is such an individual and personal acitivity, it is inevitable that any written work on the subject will reflect the views and biases of the author. In planning this book, three clearly defined needs were identified and each, in turn, has influenced the final form. First and foremost was the necessity of providing the novice with a handbook of basic information which he could assimilate and adapt to his own situation. Second, for the benefit of the wildfowler who already has years of experience tucked under the belt of his fowling smock, was the desirability of setting out some new slants on the sport without merely adding another chapter to the perpetual debate about shot sizes or choke borings. Third — and the most difficult to satisfy — was the long-felt need to make a novel breakthrough in the vexed question of wildfowl identification in wildfowling conditions.

The first demand I have attempted to meet by ordering the contents of the book in a progressive sequence and containing within each appropriate chapter enough of the elementary theory to provide the newcomer to the sport with a knowledge base upon which to build. My second aim I hope to have met by simply being myself and including sufficient personal experience and opinion to give food for thought to those readers for whom a waderful of icy brine is no new sensation.

My third purpose — to provide a useful identification key for novice and veteran alike — has been possible only with the invaluable assistance of Bernard Barker. Much of my own experience in the field of wildfowl identification has been built up over the years of listening to Bernard's theories and it was natural to turn to him for help in this context. Together we analysed the deficiencies of standard indentification plates and Bernard then designed and painted the illustrations for this book.

In essence, we sought to avoid the type of identification plate which is typified by the birdwatcher's field guide. Quite simply, ornithologists watch wildfowl in fundamentally different conditions to those experienced by the fowler and, consequently, a drawing of a duck sitting quietly on the water is of little use to the man who observes his quarry flipping past, against a murky background, in the half-light of dawn. By showing several aspects of each of the species in the I.D. plates, we hope to have provided sufficient 'keys' to enable the wildfowler to begin to compile his own databank of information through which his brain can instantaneously sort when a grey silhouette appears over the reed beds at flight time.

As mentioned previously, wildfowling is a very personal actitivity and this book inevitably tells the reader something about my own personal view of the sport. The absence of detailed reference to shooting waders, for instance, reflects not only the fact that I find great difficulty in regarding such delicate little birds as wildfowl; their omission is also designed to avoid encouraging the novice to shoot at something which he cannot positively identify. Some may not be readily mistaken but I believe that there are relatively few wildfowlers who, without really specialising in wading birds, can differentiate the few shootable species from the many protected species in the conditions which prevail on a dark estuary.

Similarly, the inclusion of chapters on gundogs and culinary practice are indicators of my opinions that no wildfowler should proceed out unless accompanied by a trained retrieving dog and that, once on the saltings, he should shoot at nothing which he, his family or his friends will not subsequently eat.

Lastly, I hope that in some small way this book imparts to the reader a notion of the romance, excitement, hardship and intrigue which — in varying proportions at different times — wildfowling has held for me since I first took down a gun and set off for the marsh.

Eric Begbie
1979

Illustration by author.

Introduction to Revised Edition

In the ten years since the original manuscript of *Modern Wildfowling* was penned there have been a number of very significant changes which have affected the wildfowler and his sport. On the legislative side the *Wildlife and Countryside Act 1981* had a marked affect, not least in terms of the restrictions which were placed upon the number of species which might legally be shot. The loss of the sea duck from the quarry list was not mourned by many wildfowlers but considerable disquiet was expressed at the protection afforded to curlew and redshank — two waders which provided very sporting shooting and appeared to be under no threat of becoming endangered species.

Other aspects of the Act were seen by wildfowlers to be plainly lunatic. Affording protection to the bean goose did little to preserve this species which, although abundant in world terms, is comparatively rare in Britain. The two main flocks of bean geese which overwinter in Britain were at little risk from wildfowlers but occasionally vagrants turn up in company with skeins of pinkfeet. The wildfowler who can positively identify a vagrant bean goose amongst a flighting skein of pinks in the gloom of a November dawn has above-average bird recognition skills. The unlucky fowler who makes this perfectly understandable mistake does, however, become an unwitting criminal.

The same situation results from the protection which is now given to the humble scaup. It is an extremely competent fowler who can differentiate a female scaup from a female tufted duck as the bird flips overhead at evening flight. The only way of avoiding a potential Court appearance is to strike the tuftie off our personal quarry lists when shooting in any location where a scaup might conceivably be encountered.

The other major legislative change has been the introduction of the *Firearms (Amendment) Act 1988*. Of most concern to the wildfowler are a number of provisions relating to the granting of a Shotgun Certificate and a restriction on the magazine capacity of semi-automatic or pump-action shotguns which might be held on a Shotgun Certificate.

Outwith the legal arena, the decade was one of growth and major change within WAGBI. In 1981 the organisation altered its name to the British

Association for Shooting and Conservation (BASC) and, partly due to the wider remit and partly because of a growing awareness amongst shooting people of the need to support an effective parliamentary lobby, its membership level accelerated beyond the 100,000 mark. Although the change of name was not universally popular amongst wildfowlers, there are few who would now deny that the organisation has continued to purposely promote the best interests of foreshore fowling.

There has also been a change in the emphasis of the research and conservation programmes promulgated by WAGBI/BASC. Up until the time of the publication of the first edition of *Modern Wildfowling* much of the conservation effort on the part of wildfowlers had been directed towards duck rearing schemes and habitat improvement. Ten years later, a considerably more scientific approach has been adopted, with lead shot poisoning research, a wildfowl disturbance study and the national shooting survey being conducted to increase the amount of reliable data which is available to further the cause of sporting shooting.

The BASC has also had to be increasingly aware of the pressures and threats which might be directed towards shooting sports from the European Parliament. To monitor and influence EEC legislation, an International Affairs section within the BASC headquarters at Marford Mill has been strengthened.

In his Foreword to the first edition of *Modern Wildfowling*, the Scottish Director of WAGBI wrote:

> 'The fowler's world of remote and windswept estuaries where geese and duck feed, where waders bustle and fill the air with their plaintive music, is one which has inspired artists and writers for centuries. The wildfowler is a lucky man and he knows it. Gradually this world is being swallowed up. The tide of industrialisation rises inexorably and takes with it the silences and the spaces. Land 'improvement' snatches at the margins and pollution sweeps into its veins. The wildfowler sees what is happening and is doing something about it.'

A feature of the 1980s was a growing political awareness of environmental issues. Perhaps we have seen the worst of the industrialisation and the pollution. Wildfowlers certainly played a crucial part in highlighting the plight of wildfowl and their reliance upon unspoiled marshes, estuaries and inland waters. Wintering populations of most of the quarry species are either stable or are enjoying an upward trend and so the fowler might be forgiven for imagining that the battles have been won and that the future of his sport is assured.

It is certainly true to suggest that wildfowling is in good heart as we approach the twenty-first century. It would be a mistake, on the other hand, to allow complacency to dull our awareness of the potential threats which do lie just beyond the horizon. Further adverse legislation must be guarded against. As mentioned already, the European situation must be kept under constant review. The acquisitive nature of some of the protectionist organisations may further reduce the amount of coastal marshland which is available for shooting.

The best possible course which the modern wildfowler can follow if he wishes to counter those dangers is to join the British Association for Shooting and Conservation and play an active role within that organisation.

Eric Begbie
1990

THE CREEKCRAWLERS

When the storm winds blow high and dawning is nigh
  And most sane folk are still fast asleep,
With a dog and a gun to the marsh they will run,
  A harvest of wildfowl to reap.

This strangely-clad crew try to stay out of view
  While they creep to the edge of the tide.
Shod in waders and wellies, they crawl on their bellies,
  To reach bank or gutter or hide.

Then when hidden from sight they will snuggle down tight,
  Out of breath and bespattered with mud,
To wait for the flight which will start at first light
  With the ducks heading back to the flood.

It's a queer kind of sport, you may hear some retort,
  To sit frozen and wet in the rain.
Masochistic's the word, for it's plainly absurd
  To get pleasure from suffering and pain.

But the fowler is tough and he's certain enough
  That it's worth waiting out on the shore,
When it's hailing or snowing and gales are a-blowing
  And the waves pound the land with a roar.

On a morning like this, it really is bliss
  To hear geese calling loud as they fly.
But if they're not wide by a mile from his hide,
  They'll be ninety yards high in the sky.

Even mallard may not give much chance of a shot
  As over the fowler they streak.
By the time he has thrown gun to shoulder they're gone,
  Just to land in the very next creek.

Though his bag may be empty, he's had chances a-plenty.
  His sport always gives him a thrill.
There is always much more than is shown by the score:
  Wildfowl ten points — wildfowlers nil.

1
The Night of the Long Guns

Brief History

The pursuit of wildfowl must be virtually as old as man himself. Wherever large flocks of geese or duck congregated, early *homo sapiens* would seek ways of coming to terms with the fowl, recognising that their value as food ranked high in the comparative order of the day. Since his most primitive beginnings man has been a hunter, the rich artwork of his early cave dwellings bearing witness to his ingenuity when it came to devising methods of trapping or killing his quarry. The club and spear were most effectively deployed against the larger mammals and, similarly, traps and pitfalls were designed, in the main, to capture ground-dwelling animals. It seems certain, however, that the cunning of our ancestors extended to taking advantage of the natural charactistics of the wildfowl family. Rounding up, clubbing or stoning during the flightless moult period, decoying or calling to within striking range of his simple weapons, netting on known flight paths — all are recorded in the annals of man's history.

By and large, those early wildfowlers practised their art to fill the bellies of their families or to barter for other necessities. Hunger rather than recreation was to remain the stimulus for most hunting pursuits until the advent of class-based civilisations in the Far East and Mediterranean regions allowed some sections of society to have leisure time at their disposal. Throughout history we find examples of entertainment and sporting diversions being based on previously necessary activities and it is no surprise to discover that the Chinese, Egyptians and Romans hunted wildfowl for pleasure. Egyptian tombs dating to 1300 BC have yielded beautifully executed paintings of young men wildfowling with S-shaped throwing sticks, geese and duck being captured with the aid of clap-nets and, perhaps most interesting of all, the use of a decoy duck fashioned out of mud and feathers.

Leaving sport aside for a moment, some particularly ingenious methods of catching duck and geese were developed and by the end of the middle ages flight-netting and decoying were common in Europe. Without doubt the most productive of all was the decoy pond which originated in the Netherlands and was adopted for use in England and elsewhere.

The decoy pond consists of an open pool from which radiates a number

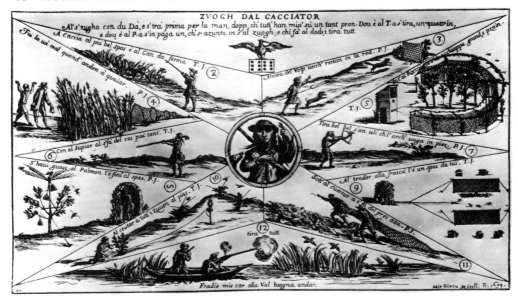

The game of the hunter. As far back as 1699, wildfowling held pride of place amongst field sports. *(Photograph courtesy: Jim Humphreys)*

of curving channels or pipes. Each pipe is covered by netting and tapers away from the pond to end in a catching bag or cage. Tame duck or food are used to attract wild birds to the pool whereupon they are lured up one of the pipes by the use of a fox-like dog which is traditionally named 'Piper'. A series of screens along the length of the pipe permits the decoyman to control his dog without being seen and, by using the natural tendency of duck to group together and mob a fox-like animal, the fowl are gradually led away from the central pond and into the catching bag. Huge quantities of duck were once caught in this way in order to supply the city markets, one Dutch decoy accounting for over 25,000 birds in a single year. Few now operate commercially but a number are maintained and used for research and ringing purposes.

Firearms

In seeking the origins of the modern sport of wildfowling we must turn our attention to the development of firearms. The gun is perhaps unique in the history of early weapons in that it was designed and improved primarily for military purposes. Almost without exception, earlier killing instruments such as the spear and bow were first used for hunting, their employment in man-to-man hostilities developing later. It was the medieval armourers, however, who were responsible for the evolution of the gun, and its widespread use for peaceful purposes appears to have been delayed until the sixteenth century, by which time the matchlock had been perfected.

Even at this stage, no fast-moving target was in much danger and, whereas a hungry peasant might well take a shot at a flock of sitting birds, the Tudor sportsmen preferred the longbow or crossbow when seeking diversion in the green fields and forests of England. Early in the seventeenth century the invention of the flintlock made wing-shooting a practicable proposition but for some time yet the slaying of fowl with a gun was to be regarded as a method of filling the pot rather than as a sporting pastime. Indeed, the gentry with their bows, dogs and nets looked down upon the early gunners and one finds many examples of statutes and bye-laws which were designed to restrict shooting to an extent which could hardly be justified on the grounds of conservation!

One early Hampshire bye-law, dated 1634, was clearly intended to curb the enthusiasm of wildfowlers, although it is unlikely that the brent geese (Brangesse) were in any danger of extinction in that year:

> 'We sett a paine uppon all those that shall heereafter use to shoote with fowling peeces or other small peeces at any Brangesse or other fowle at or neere the round tower.'

The sportsmen of continental Europe appear to have been somewhat more favourably disposed towards firearms than their British counterparts. There is a wealth of information in written form and also in paintings, drawings and engravings which suggests that the period between 1650 and 1750 witnessed an upsurge of interest in shooting game and fowl in France, Italy and Spain. The original print which is illustrated on page 18 has been framed and hangs on the wall of a sitting room in Kent. It was not intended to be a decoration, however, its Italian designer setting it out as a board game to be played with dice on a 'put or take' basis. It is of particular interest that in 1699 the winning position of the game was illustrated by the pursuit of wildfowl. In the north of Italy, at least, shooting duck was considered to be a superior sport to netting, trapping or decoying.

Wildfowling in Britain

It is difficult to pinpoint just when wildfowling became widespread in Britain but there is no doubt that by the closing decades of the eighteenth century there were men who shot geese and duck to supply the markets and feed their families. The years between 1760 and 1850 were noted for the contrast, and occasionally conflict, which existed between the professional fowler and the gentleman sportsman. Both used muzzle-loading flintlocks or percussion guns, both employed punts and swivel guns to pursue large flocks of fowl and each regarded the other with a measure of disdain. Apart from a common interest in shooting wildfowl, their respective ways of life could hardly have been farther apart.

This was the age of the wild marshman, the fen tiger who fished and speared eels in summer and stalked geese on the saltings in winter. The literature may be over-romantic but it abounds with images of gnarled, hard men toting their long 'marsh rails' with sixty-inch barrels in pursuit of great clouds of fowl which reputedly blackened the sky. Certainly the marshes of Hampshire and Kent, of Norfolk and Lincolnshire, the estuaries of Scotland and the loughs of Ireland all harboured teeming populations of duck and geese which could be harvested by those who knew the gutters and creeks, who lived with the wild wind and weather and tides. The reek of black powder from an eight-bore shoulder piece, or the boom and belch of flame from the two-inch barrel of a mighty punt gun, were part of the lonely life of those worthies in the days long before the invention of the motor car or the spread of the railway.

Picture, if you can, a marshland scene from those years. Living in a small cottage of dry stone and peat with an earthen floor and an open fire, the fisherman-fowler eked out a bare existence by pitting his not inconsiderable wits against the wild creatures which he found in the sedge-lined fens or the water meadows. Although Adam Smith had published his work *The Wealth of Nations* in 1776, the concept of the division of labour was totally alien to the men who lived on marsh and shore. Each season brought a different group of tasks to be undertaken. Gathering peewit eggs, catching pike and perch, trapping eels, netting plover, digging turf, shooting wild-fowl — each had its place in the countryman's year and each demanded a skill which was passed from father to son over countless generations.

Colonel Peter Hawker (1786–1853).

(Taken from *Instructions to Young Sportsmen*.)

It was the fowling which demanded the greatest hardiness. When fresh-water lakes were covered by ice and the turf and peat were frozen solid, it was to the saltings that the duck punts were taken and with stanchion gun or eight-bore the flocks of wigeon, brent, mallard and pinkfeet were relent-lessly hunted. The racing seas and storm winds of an east coast winter were hazards which simply had to be faced if a bag of fowl was to be made and the brown-faced men with their leather hip-boots, moleskin caps and damascus barrels did not shy from the task.

A Gentleman Gunner — Colonel Peter Hawker

While the poor men with their nets and lines and long guns sought to scrape a living from the harvest of fish and fowl, a few gentlefolk were attracted by the challenges of fen and saltmarsh. Best known and most quoted of the early gentlemen-gunners was Colonel Peter Hawker who recorded in his shooting diaries a wealth of detail concerning his sport. Even in Hawker's day wildfowling was not quite respectable and his work *Instructions to Young Sportsmen* probably did much to popularise the pursuit amongst the gentry and rising middle classes. His famous double punt gun performed considerable execution amongst the fowl of Southampton Water and the Solent, as the following extract from one day of his diary certifies:

'The "Lion" punt brought them to action at last! All I got on the spot, however, was thirty-two wigeon, two mallards, and a coot (at one shot), but including what other people got and brought me, I had killed — fifty-three wigeon, two mallards, and a coot at one shot! The greatest work that ever has been done here!

'To make this brilliant shot the more extraordinary I should name that it was done about half past twelve in the day. The gunners to windward had driven all the birds down to Keyhaven, and they congregated (about 1,000 strong) just off "Shorehead" in the shallow water, and, by having a favourable time, I just slipped into them before the other gunners could get up.

'In the afternoon I had only just come in to refresh myself and wipe the gun. Off again at ten, out all night, and the severest night I ever remembered. My cap froze to my head, and it blew a gale of wind; but I had so much to do that I perspired the whole time, except at intervals when my hands were so frost-bitten that it was with the utmost difficulty I could grope out the traps to load, and particularly to prime the gun. The man who followed me, as dead bird-picker, fell over-board and was obliged to go home (in order to avoid being frozen to death), and I thus lost at least a third of my birds which fell in the hands of the leeward shore-hunters who lurk about, after gunners, as vultures follow an army, at all hours of the day and night when there is a hard frost and a chance of a good plunder. The labour of working the fowl was an odd mixture of ecstasy and slavery. I brought home (shot on the spot and caught on the ice at daybreak by self and helpers) sixty-nine wigeon and a duck! — making in all 101 wigeon, and four duck and mallards (beside six plover and the old coot) in eighteen hours! — as I was out from past twelve in the day till six the next morning. The gun missed fire twice, owing to the elastic fluid being frozen, and I missed one fine shot owing to the spray of the sea freezing on the punt and forming a mass of ice that threw the night-level far above its bearings. My best shot of the night (or rather at two in the morning) was thirty wigeon with one barrel. The left barrel snapped, as the lock had broken again (but on getting home to the candle I luckily found it was not so far gone but that I could make shift with it, on being a little rectified).

'Had not this misfortune occurred, and my follower remained, I really believe I should at least have doubled what I did!'

The Sportsman-Naturalist

From the 1850s until the turn of the century, wildfowling continued to be both a commercial activity and a sport of gentlemen. Despite Hawker's preoccupation with 'lowzy tailors' and 'tit-shooters' there was still plenty of space on the shores of Britain and more than enough fowl to go round. The

The sport of gentlemen. H.R.H. The Prince of Wales shooting geese around 1880.

advent of the breech-loading shotgun undoubtedly assisted the coastal gunner, and improved communications permitted fowling expeditions to be planned and effected with greater ease. For the broadsman and his contemporaries there was little change in the fowling scene but in the towns and the cities a new breed was emerging — the sportsman-naturalist. On the unspoiled wetlands of Britain, as in the jungles and savannahs of Africa, hunting was becoming allied to the collection and study of wildlife specimens. They started young in those days. John Guille Millais commenced shooting and collecting at the age of eleven and by the time he was sixteen he had three times walked the east coast of Scotland from Dunbar in the south to Thurso in the north, equipped with only his gun and a bag of clothing.

This, too, was the era of Sir Ralph Payne-Gallwey, Abel Chapman and a youthful Stanley Duncan, all of whom made substantial contributions to the sport of wildfowling and recorded their experiences for future generations. In their heyday, fowl would appear to have been just as plentiful as when Hawker wrote his diaries and some large bags were made and committed to the record books. In this extract from *The Wildfowler in Scotland*, Millais describes an exciting duck flight:

'The best day's shooting at mallard that ever fell to my lot was on Loch Leven. On December 13, 1885, I went there with Mr Malloch on one of my usual winter visits to shoot and collect birds. We had hardly started with the boat, rowing close to the Castle Island, when a gale sprang up from the south-west and set every duck on the great lake flying about and moving for shelter; and now, seeing that a good many birds were apparently pitching fairly close in to the Castle Island, we landed, I going to the north and my companion ensconcing himself at another point. A good many duck soon commenced to alight, but nearly all just out of shot; when, chancing to turn and look through the trees, I saw that many more were sheltering immediately under the Reed Bower, a small island close by, covered with trees and heavy undergrowth. There we made our way, and I landed while Mr Malloch went off in the boat, to the far end of the lake, to see what he could do by lying-up on the Inch, another favoured shelter some two miles away. Hardly had he taken his departure when a small bunch of mallard came in close to my shelter and I got a brace of them. In a minute or two another lot made their appearance, till "thick and fast they came at last, and more and more and more". I have never in my life had such continuous banging at one stand — at duck at any rate. At intervals of every few minutes two or three little grey specks would appear away down wind, and would presently look bigger and bigger. As soon as these birds saw my three pneumatic decoys I had anchored out to attract them, there was a sudden movement of recognition, a dropping of wings, a clamour of welcome, and then, as they were about to alight, I would show myself, and as they shot upwards again blaze away. After about two hours of excellent sport, "Jet" who was the most gallant of water-dogs, began to show signs of cramp, which was not surprising, seeing that almost every duck she fetched from the water meant one hundred and fifty yards swim against (even under this comparative shelter) a heavy head wind, and on a bitterly cold day . . . The mallard continued to come in till three in the afternoon, when Mr Malloch appeared, having shot twenty-five duck on the west end of the Inch, where, he said, the birds had come in well. For me, "Jet" had recovered from the waters fifty-six mallard and four teal, and as the storm had somewhat abated we made for the lee shore to pick up my drifters . . . Thus actually were shot on this great day 108 mallard and teal, all of which, except the damaged birds, were taken home and made use of.'

Fresh water perhaps, but Millais certainly makes Loch Leven sound every bit as wild as his beloved east coast estuaries. Indeed, storms, gales and danger appear throughout his writing and even sheltered waters such as the Eden estuary at St Andrews succeeded in testing his skill and hardiness as he punted his way through squall and ice-flow.

The Eden Estuary where Millais used to shoot with his punt gun.

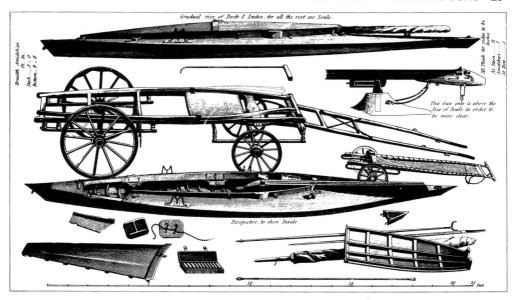

Punt and gear for 200 lb gun. (Taken from *Instructions to Young Sportsmen*.)

WAGBI

The opening years of the twentieth century were to be critical in the history of wildfowling. While game shooting passed from strength to strength and grouse, pheasant and partridge continued to rain down around the guns of moor, field and covert, some sensitive individuals began to detect a wind of change blowing into the marshes and fens of Britain. Drainage was beginning to endanger a number of prime wetland areas, more and more Guns were appearing on the saltings and, most sinister of all, a movement of opposition to fieldsports was germinating in the urban centres of population. Times were becoming harder for the professional fowler and intellectual extremists were challenging the ethics of the sport.

Conscious of the threat which hung over the future of wildfowling, Stanley Duncan convened a meeting of friends in his hut at Patrington Haven near Hull in 1908. As a result of that gathering of enthusiasts the Wildfowlers' Association of Great Britain and Ireland (WAGBI) was inaugurated with Sir Ralph Payne-Gallwey as president and Duncan as honorary secretary.

Change there would be; the night of the long guns had all but ended and a new generation of wildfowlers was about to be born. Guarded and guided by the Wildfowlers' Association, they would face the challenges of the twentieth century — challenges posed by the pace of agricultural and industrial development, by the threat of pollution and by the social consequences of the internal combustion engine.

2
The Age of Enlightenment

The good old days or the bad old days? When one reads the histories of wildfowlers and wildfowling it is difficult to decide. Admittedly the fens, backwaters and estuaries were largely unspoiled and it is true that the abundance of wetland habitat supported a large and prolific wildfowl population. Moreover, it cannot be doubted that there was romance and excitement aplenty for those who had the means to shoot for sport with punt or shoulder gun. But what of the professional fowler? Was he really a figure to be envied as he struggled to subsist in his broken-down cottage, as he faced wind and weather, not from choice but of necessity, probably crippled by lumbago or rheumatism in early middle age? I suspect that while many of today's sportsmen would happily spend a week or two exposed to his hardships and poor conditions, few would elect to commit themselves totally to this way of life.

The ethics and conduct of the old wildfowlers were also more than a trifle at variance with those which are almost universally accepted today. Larger and larger bags were sought after and the rarer the bird, the more desirable was its killing. With a very few notable exceptions, the shore gunners and punters of yesteryear pursued their quarry completely oblivious to the long-term effects of their activities. Avocet, bittern, reeve and phalarope were prizes to be valued if they came within gunshot range.

That state of affairs simply could not continue. As the marshes were drained and industry claimed prime sites on the estuaries of Britain, the future of many species was placed in jeopardy. As modern transport enabled the townsman to seek recreation on the shores of our island, so did shooting pressure dramatically increase. In the aftermath of each global conflict came a heightened public awareness of the dangers facing wildlife and renewed demands for total protection. Against this background, the sport of wildfowling changed gradually to accommodate the altered circumstances and, over three-quarters of a century, fowlers adapted their ways in recognition of the twin needs of habitat preservation and wildfowl conservation.

This transformation was not sudden and throughout the period there was a considerable overlap between the old-timers and the modern thinkers. Some noteworthy conversions occurred as individual fowlers

Puntgunning. (Taken from *Instructions to Young Sportsmen.*)

came to realise that mass killing could not go on forever. One of the best-documented cases is that of Kenzie Thorpe, who acted as guide and general labourer to a young Peter Scott.

Kenzie Thorpe and Sir Peter Scott

Born in 1908, Kenzie Thorpe was a hard man in many senses of the words. A combination of the blood of a pure romany father and a Lincolnshire mother, he poached hare and pheasant from the grand estates of the area and shot geese and duck on the coastal marshes. Before World War II, he was signed up by Peter Scott to assist with the maintenance of a small wildfowl collection at Scott's lighthouse home near Sutton Bridge. Not that this liaison put an end to Thorpe's wild exploits. He continued to pay fines and even serve a short prison sentence in consequence of shooting forays which failed to remain within the constraints of the law. In the latter years of his life, however, Kenzie Thorpe did appear to repent and become a responsible wildfowling guide and a supporter of WAGBI. For many wild-fowlers, their last memory of 'Kenzie the Wild Goose Man' will be his wildfowl-calling demonstrations on the WAGBI stand at Game Fairs.

The conversion of Peter Scott himself was no less noteworthy. In 1927, at the age of eighteen, Scott went up to Trinity College, Cambridge, to read Natural Sciences and, within a month, found himself frequenting the washes of the fenland rivers with his father's little-used Cogswell & Harrison shotgun. It did not take long for the wildfowling bug to grip firmly at his youthful fancy and by Christmas of the same year he was punt-ing through the marshes in pursuit of mallard and wigeon. On 6 February 1928 Scott's first goose — ironically a relatively rare bean goose — hit the mud at Terrington Wash, the forerunner of many hundreds which were to meet a similar fate as he gunned his way around Britain and Europe. The enthusiasm with which he engaged in wildfowling was quite remarkable and by 1932 he was already showing an interest in capturing geese alive as well as in shooting them.

When *Morning Flight* was published in 1935 there were signs that Scott was clearly experiencing a measure of remorse at the large bags of geese which he had taken and from that time until wartime duties claimed his attentions he was shooting with a greater degree of moderation. Throughout those years his collection of wildfowl grew, as did his fame as an artist. From the lighthouse studio near Sutton Bridge flowed a stream of paintings, many of which embodied the very essence of time and tide, storm and saltmarsh, distilled from his experiences in the creeks and channels of the Wash.

Sir Peter Scott did, of course, become best known to the British public as founder of the Wildlife Trust, rather than as a wildfowler or painter. The Trust does a great deal of valuable work in relation to wildfowl conservation but it is perhaps a little ironic that its policies are not always seen to be totally sympathetic towards the modern wildfowler — despite the fact that the shore gunner of today is likely to pursue his sport in a much more moderate and responsible way than was characterised by the early career of Scott himself.

Legislative Change

The literature of the middle years of the twentieth century differs markedly from that of a hundred years earlier. Wentworth Day, 'BB', Sedgwick and Cadman all stressed the qualities of sportsmanship, fieldsmanship, restraint and respect, rather than dwelling upon detailed accounts of massive kills. The tide was turning for wildfowl and wildfowler alike. In the event, the change of attitude towards the sport probably saved wildfowling in Britain from some of the heavy restrictions which were considered necessary in the United States. As early as 1865 the American fowler found his punt gun and swivel gun banned by law. In 1919 the use of guns larger than ten-bore was outlawed, and by 1925 a daily bag limit of fifteen birds was in force. So endangered became the migratory wildfowl of North America that very short shooting seasons and positive management quotas became necessary. Today, despite the obvious success of many of the management strategies, waterfowling in the USA remains subject to the scientifically derived restrictions which seek to balance the annual harvest of duck and geese with breeding success. Not that all is gloomy on the other side of the Atlantic — at least the Stateside duck hunter has the satisfaction of knowing that the revenues from his Duck Stamps and hunting licences are used for waterfowl conservation and the development of his sport.

Legislation in Britain has been moderate by comparison. In 1954 the *Protection of Birds Act* was passed and in 1968 a *Firearms Act* was added to the statute book but attempts during the committee stages of those Acts to ban punt gunning or to seriously restrict the ownership of shotguns were successfully defeated. Threats to wildfowling were also presented during the framing of the *Wildlife and Countryside Act 1981* and the *Firearms (Amendment) Act 1988* and, although some concessions were made, many of the worst potential effects of both pieces of legislation were avoided.

Industrialisation has reduced the amount of wildfowl habitat on many estuaries.

The Growth of WAGBI/BASC

To a very large extent, the shape of wildfowling in Britain has been determined by the Wildfowlers' Association. WAGBI, as it was known until 1981, was not only the fowler's watchdog when threats loomed on the horizon, but the organisation also successfully fostered meaningful co-operation between shooting and conservation interests. The essence of this partnership was encapsulated in a booklet, *The Story of a Triumvirate*, published jointly by the Nature Conservancy, WAGBI and the Wildfowl Trust in 1970. The major growth of the Association has occurred since 1950 and there are now hundreds of affiliated clubs, syndicates and supporter organisations which carry the message to and from local level. With over

100,000 members, and now known as the British Association for Shooting and Conservation, it is represented upon many important national and international committees and works very hard indeed for the British sportsman.

Having outgrown offices in Liverpool and Chester, the BASC now operates from a splendid centre at Marford Mill in North Wales, where an enthusiastic and dedicated staff actively promote the aims which were first spelled out by Stanley Duncan in 1908. For the member, either directly or through a local club, there is a wealth of advice, information and assistance available covering all aspects of wildfowling, gameshooting, practical conservation and firearms law. Without exception, every fowler in this country should be a member of this fine organisation.

Great Black-backed gulls moving wigeon. (Taken from *The Wildfowler in Scotland.*)

One can look to all sorts of theories to explain the enlightened approach of wildfowlers in the twentieth century — the social levelling which occurred during and after the Great War, the determination of all sections of society to stamp out extreme poverty or the revolutions in education and social welfare which followed World War II. Improvements in communication played their part — the spread of radio, television and, indeed, universal literacy undoubtedly opened the eyes of a growing public to the plight of wildlife in this country. Above all, however, I suspect that knowledge and circumstances brought to the surface the innate love and respect which the hunter has always held for his quarry. As economic change squeezed the market gunner from the scene, the sportsman was left to rule the marshes and he was increasingly conscious of the need to conserve the wildfowl populations and protect as much of the wetland habitat as could be saved. It would be wrong to think of the BASC as an impersonal bureaucratic entity issuing edicts to control and restrict the activities of wildfowlers. The Association is comprised of sportsmen and its initiatives in the fields of shooting conduct and conservation stem directly from the self-perceived needs and aspirations of the fowlers themselves.

Teal. (Taken from *The Wildfowler in Scotland.*)

From the previous dichotomy of gentleman punter and peasant gunner has developed a broad-based, well-regulated sport, the exponents of which are as critically aware of the future as they are of the past. That is not to say that there is no place for nostalgia. At the end of the day, the intimate relationship between individual wildfowler and his quarry out there in the solitude of a dawning estuary has changed little. By constant vigilance and readiness to meet and adapt to the challenges of the day, may that primordial magic be with us for a very long time to come.

3
Wildfowling Today

As the twentieth century draws towards its close, the wildfowler must, perforce, face problems of a nature and magnitude which would not have been dreamed of by his predecessors in the sport. No longer does the longshore gunner have total freedom of the saltings and an abundance of wildfowl blackening the sky above every estuary. To secure worthwhile sport the modern wildfowler must either be prepared to co-operate with his fellows in fowling clubs and associations or — a diminishing alternative — seek out one of the very few remaining foreshores which have escaped the attentions of the motorised hordes.

The Law

Before considering the question of finding a place to shoot, it is necessary to be clear about one or two of the statutory limitations which impinge upon the activities of the wildfowler. In the first instance, any person who wishes to own or use a shotgun in Britain is governed by the *Firearms Act 1968* and the *Firearms (Amendment) Act 1988*. Under this legislation a shotgun is defined as a smooth-bore gun, not being an airgun, having a barrel length of not less than twenty-four inches. To purchase, acquire or possess such a weapon a person must hold a current Shotgun Certificate which is obtained by application on the prescribed form to the Chief Constable of the applicant's home area. A gun cannot be held on a Shotgun Certificate if it has a magazine which can hold more than two cartridges. If it has a magazine which, after manufacture, has been adapted to hold no more than two cartridges, then the adaptation must be certified as such by a Proof House.

The Chief Constable may refuse to issue a Shotgun Certificate if he is satisfied that an applicant does not have a good reason for possessing a gun or cannot be permitted to possess one without danger to public safety or to the peace. A Shotgun Certificate will specify the description of the shotguns to which it relates and this will include, where known, the identification numbers of the guns. Under the rules pertaining to Shotgun Certificates, the owner of a gun is required to ensure its safekeeping when not in use and to notify the police of any change of permanent address.

To purchase shotgun ammunition, it is necessary to produce a Shotgun

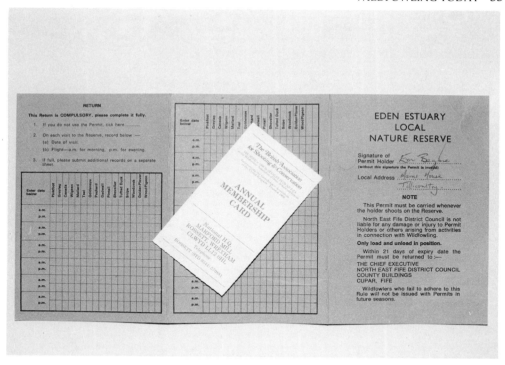

On some estuaries permits may be required.

Certificate together with written permission from the certificate holder if the ammunition is not being purchased by the holder in person.

These requirements are considerably stricter than the situation prior to 1968, when, for the price of a few shillings, anyone could obtain a gun licence over the counter of his local Post Office. By and large, however, the country sports community has accepted such restrictions with equanimity although, in the main, new legislation has been promulgated by governments wishing to allay public anxiety about law and order — anxiety which would have been better directed towards the criminal fraternity rather than law-abiding sportsmen.

Bird Protection

The law as it affects the wildfowler's quarry is mainly contained within the *Wildlife and Countryside Act 1981*, the basic principle of which is that all wild birds, together with their nests and eggs, are fully protected. It is the specified exceptions to the Act which allow shooting of certain species to take place at stated times of the year. When looking back to the days of Hawker and Millais, the wildfowler of today may feel that his shooting season is unduly short and his quarry list greatly curtailed but, with the exception of a few contentious species such as the brent goose, curlew and redshank, there is general agreement that the legislation is reasonably fair.

The species of duck and geese which the wildfowler may legally hunt outside the close season are defined in Part I of Schedule 2 of the *Wildlife and Countryside Act 1981*. They are as follows:

Canada Goose	Pochard
Gadwall	Shoveler
Goldeneye	Teal
Greylag Goose	Tufted Duck
Mallard	Whitefronted Goose
Pinkfooted Goose	(in England and Wales only)
Pintail	Wigeon

Of the species, other than duck and geese, which are also contained within Part I of Schedule 2 of the *Wildlife and Countryside Act 1981* the following will be encountered upon some coastal marsh areas and for that reason may be of interest to the wildfowler:

Common Snipe	Golden Plover
Woodcock	

Coot and moorhen are contained within the same list but neither are normally considered to be quarry species, although in bygone times large-scale coot shoots were practised in some parts of the country. The final species to be found in Part I of Schedule 2 is the capercaillie and this bird is not, of course, an inhabitant of the foreshore.

Part II of the same schedule contains those birds which do not enjoy a close season and may be shot by authorised persons throughout the year. Although none is classified as wildfowl, several are regarded as worthy quarry by the all-round sportsman and a number may be culled for pest-control purposes. Those of most concern to the reader of this book are likely to be:

Crow	Jay
Collared Dove	Magpie
Feral Pigeon	Rook
Jackdaw	Woodpigeon

Close Seasons

Above high water mark the statutory close season for wild duck and geese is from 1 February until 31 August, both dates inclusive. On the foreshore the close season for those species runs from 21 February until 31 August. This means that the wildfowler may pursue his quarry from 1 September of any year until 31 January of the following year and that, so long as he remains on the designated foreshore area, he may extend his shooting season until 20 February. It is important to note, however, that the fore-shore extension to the shooting season applies only to duck and geese and not, for instance, to golden plover.

For the sake of completeness, it may be noted that the close season for woodcock runs from 1 February to 30 September in England and Wales, and until 31 August in Scotland. Common snipe has a close season from 1 February until 11 August.

Apart from the statutory close seasons, it is illegal to shoot Schedule 2 birds on Christmas Day throughout England, Scotland and Wales and to shoot Schedule 2, Part I, birds on Sundays in Scotland and certain counties and county boroughs of England and Wales. Those areas are:

Anglesey	Great Yarmouth
Brecknock	Isle of Ely
Caernarvon	Leeds
Cardigan	Merioneth
Carmarthen	Norfolk
Cornwall	Pembroke
Denbigh	Somerset
Devon	Yorkshire (North Riding)
Doncaster	Yorkshire (West Riding)
Glamorgan	

It will be noted, however, that many of the above named are areas which ceased to have discrete administrative status at the time of local government reorganisation in 1974. Some confusion exists as to the precise position relating to Sunday wildfowling in some of the counties and the prudent fowler will be well advised to check with his own local council.

Foreshore

The firearms law and the general conservation legislation applies equally throughout England, Wales and Scotland. Given that most wildfowling takes place below the sea wall, however, it is important to note that the legal definition of foreshore, together with rules about access, differ significantly between England and Wales on the one hand and Scotland on the other. Consequently, to avoid confusion, it is necessary to set out the respective situations separately.

England and Wales

The case of *Beckett v. Lyons (1967) 1 AER 833* finally dispelled the myth that, in England and Wales, there was a public right to shoot on the foreshore. It follows, therefore, that any person who takes a shotgun on to the shore without proper authorisation not only renders himself liable to a civil action for trespass but, under the *Firearms Act 1968*, makes himself liable to prosecution for the criminal offence of armed trespass.

Members of the British Association for Shooting and Conservation are in a somewhat privileged position in that much of the area below high water mark is owned by the Crown or the Duchy of Lancaster and, except where the sporting rights have been let to a third party, the BASC has obtained an agreement that its members will not be prosecuted for armed trespass if they resort to such foreshore for the purpose of wildfowling.

That having been said, the reality of the situation is that the most worthwhile areas of fowling marsh have been leased by wildfowling clubs, are in private ownership or have been designated as nature reserves. In consequence, there are few areas of England and Wales where an itinerant gunner can simply cross the sea wall and obtain good quality sport without the need to acquire a permit.

In England and Wales the foreshore is defined as that area which is more often than not covered by the flux and reflux of the four ordinary tides occurring midway between springs and neaps. In effect, therefore, much of the prime wildfowling land which is flooded by only the highest spring tides does not fall within that area which is classified as foreshore and the fowler will be committing an offence if he shoots from such salt marsh without specific permission from the owner.

Scotland

In Scotland the situation is somewhat different from that in England and Wales. Although the *Firearms Act 1968* applies equally in Scotland, there is considered to be a public right to carry a gun on the foreshore for the purpose of wildfowling and, hence, the offence of armed trespass is not committed by the fowler who enters such an area without express permission. This situation arises because in Scotland, irrespective of ownership, the Crown has retained certain rights in respect of the foreshore and holds those in trust for the public. Despite this general rule, many of the best areas of wildfowling foreshore in Scotland are now effectively controlled as a result of the creation of nature reserves with wildfowling permit schemes. On other parts of the Scottish coast there may remain a public right to shoot but access to the high water mark is restricted by the owners of adjacent land. Only where an established *right of way* exists does the fowler have a right to cross private land in order to gain access to the foreshore.

The definition of foreshore differs in Scotland and is considerably more favourable to the wildfowler. That area which lies between the high and low water marks of ordinary spring tides is classified as foreshore and consequently includes areas of saltings and merse which would be excluded by the definition pertaining in England and Wales.

Other Legal Requirements

No Game Licence is required to shoot wild geese and duck. If, however, the wildfowler intends to shoot any game species, such as snipe or woodcock, then a Game Licence must first be obtained from a Post Office.

The *Wildlife and Countryside Act 1981* prohibits the sale of dead wild geese at any time. Dead wild duck may only be sold between 1 September and 28 February.

The Act also prohibits certain methods of killing or taking wildfowl. Of most importance to the wildfowler are:

a) By using any automatic weapon or any semi-automatic weapon with a magazine capacity of more than two rounds.

b) By using any shotgun of which the barrel has an internal diameter at the muzzle in excess of one and three-quarter inches.

c) The use of any device for illuminating a target.

d) The use of any form of artificial lighting or any mirror or other dazzling device.

e) The use as a decoy of any sound recording, or any tethered or injured live bird or animal.

f) The use of any mechanically propelled vehicle or boat in the immediate pursuit of a wild bird.

Under exceptional circumstances, for instance a period of prolonged severe weather or serious pollution, the Secretary of State may issue an Order affording additional protection to specified species of wild birds. In relation to hard weather suspensions of wildfowl shooting, the Secretary of State will be expected to act in accordance with procedures and criteria which have been agreed between the Nature Conservancy Council and the BASC.

Where to Shoot?

Having familiarised himself with all the legal restrictions which will impose upon his pursuit of duck and geese, the apprentice wildfowler is faced with the much more practical problem of finding somewhere to shoot. It is important to stress at this stage the very considerable advantages which are to be derived from membership of the BASC and one of its affiliated clubs. Although such a step may not immediately open the door to much shooting, it will put the newcomer in touch with experienced fowlers.

It is incumbent upon the novice, therefore, to gain the trust and respect of the veterans he encounters; not an easy task but one in which humility and a demonstrated eagerness to learn will pay dividends. So, too, will a willingness to volunteer for any work which the club requires to be done. Days spent digging ponds, felling trees, planting verges or simply address-ing envelopes will ultimately be rewarded with a scrap of information or

The B.A.S.C. headquarters at Marford Mill.

even an occasional invitation to accompany a more experienced fowler on a morning flight.

In England and Wales, many of the best wildfowling marshes are controlled — or even owned — by fowling clubs, and members have controlled access for shooting. Some of these clubs also operate permit systems which allow other BASC members to shoot on a day-ticket basis. Details of permit schemes can be obtained from BASC offices.

In Scotland it is not possible for wildfowling clubs to own or lease the shooting rights on the foreshore and, for this reason, some clubs have sought to have nature reserves established with controlled wildfowling operating under permit schemes. Once again, particulars of permits can be obtained from the BASC. Elsewhere in Scotland the right to shoot wildfowl below high water mark is free and this freedom is jealously guarded by many fowlers.

Such guidance is all very well for the person who has the good fortune to reside within striking distance of a suitable wildfowling shoreline. There are many, on the other hand, for whom shooting wildfowl can only come at the culmination of a carefully planned expedition to some distant estuary. The man who leaves his office or factory on a Friday afternoon, packs gun, dog and the other accoutrements of his sport into a car and then sets out on a journey of several hundred miles, must seek to establish contacts in his chosen hunting ground which will permit him to obtain news of the fowling prospects and guidance in respect of the movements of the fowl.

Careful Planning

Good planning can really make all the difference between the success or failure of a fowling trip. For a number of years I had the good fortune to meet two Humberside lads each season. Yapper Mike and Oil Can John earned their nicknames amongst the fisher-folk and both were very experienced fowlers. They made at least one visit to the Tay estuary each winter and the timing of their arrival was computed with extraordinary accuracy to take maximum advantage from the phase of the moon, the times of high tide and the height of the tide. One year, in particular, the rewards of their attention to detail were evident for all to see.

It had been a mild, wet autumn with very little in the way of stormy weather to set a wildfowler's pulse racing. October and November passed without any memorable flights being experienced in eastern Scotland and so poor were the prospects that the local men were more inclined to go pigeon and rabbit shooting than to seek their sport on the foreshore. Then, about ten days before Christmas, I received a phone call from Mike to say that he and his pal were arriving that night and hoped that I could join them for a dawn flight at Kingoodie Bay.

Pleased that they were coming north but uncertain as to whether they would find their journey worthwhile, I prepared my gun and waterproofs before going to bed and set the alarm clock for five-thirty. I need not have bothered with the latter. At around two o'clock in the morning I was awakened by the spiteful rattle of rain being blown against my bedroom window and for the next three hours lay listening to the howl of a rising gale. No wildfowler can sleep at times like that and I was out of bed, washed, shaved and breakfasted long before the time came to release my labradors from their kennel and point the car up the M90 motorway.

When I met John and Mike at the Invergowrie road end, they were already anticipating some fine sport. During the night the weather had steadily worsened and we had to strain our ears to discern the occasional fragment of goose-talk above the wailing of the wind which flattened the reedbeds around the bay.

The sky was slow to lighten that morning but, as dawn finally broke, the greylag skeins forsook the sanctuary of the distant saltings and battled inland in the teeth of the north-easter. We all stopped shooting well before the flight was over — to have done otherwise would have been greedy despite the poor returns from earlier outings that season. In any case, both the Hull fowlers reckoned that three or four geese apiece was sufficient recompense for a 500-mile round trip.

The point of the story is that Mike explained to me later that morning that he had developed an almost infallible system for planning their forays. He had a wall planner at home upon which the times of full and new moon, together with the quarters, were marked. Also charted was the tide information for three wildfowling sites — the Tay and Solway estuaries and the Wash. By careful attention to the coastal shipping weather forecasts, he could be warned of approaching storms and then work out whether the best chance of encountering favourable tides lay north, south or west. He had also known that on the morning in question the prospects would be better on the north side of the Tay rather than on the opposite shore.

Not all wildfowlers reap the benefits of such careful preparation. Living close to three major fowling estuaries, I witness an annual influx of visitors who have embarked upon their expedition without adequate preparation and who, as a result, enjoy very little sport. Regrettably, much of the unsporting behaviour which occurs on the foreshore arises, I suspect, from the frustration of constantly being in the wrong place at the wrong time; frustration which could have been minimalised if only a little advance planning had preceded the trip. Already there have been examples of wild-fowling clubs closing their foreshores to all visitors due to misbehaviour on the part of a small minority. It is a fact, however, that poor conduct reflects badly upon the entire fowling community.

Wildfowlers planning a journey to a strange area may find hoteliers and publicans to be a useful source of knowledge and no expedition should be embarked upon without first making contact with the secretary of the local wildfowling club. However, the real gems of assistance are most likely to come from local fowlers who have become genuine friends over a period of years. Once again the novice is in the position of having to build up the trust and respect of hitherto strangers; a task at which some are better able than others.

It should also be borne in mind that the necessary access permissions should be obtained in advance. Authority to cross private land cannot normally be obtained at four o'clock on a winter's morning. Nor should it be assumed that permission granted in a previous year will still be valid. A survey of the area in daylight will alert the fowler to any hazards which might cause difficulty in the dark and will also provide the opportunity to check out other little practical points such as the parking places which will not inconvenience farm workers when they start to go about their daily toil.

The Importance of Courtesy

There are a number of basic courtesies which must be observed if one wishes to be welcomed back to any area. The considerate wildfowler, for instance, will not slam car doors nor cause any other unnecessary noise in the early hours of the morning. It is essential to ensure that guns are covered and dogs — however well trained — are restrained on a lead while

Self restraint is particularly important when decoying geese on their feeding grounds.

crossing private ground. In this manner one will avoid any misunderstanding with landowners or gamekeepers. Mention of gamekeepers brings to mind a vital point concerning pheasants and partridges. In certain circumstances it may be lawful to shoot a game bird which flies over the wildfowler's position on the foreshore. Lawful — but certainly not prudent. The farmer who generously granted permission to cross his land will be very likely to withdraw it if he sees his pheasants being shot on the adjacent saltings by the fowlers to whom he extended the privilege of access.

Ethics and conduct are increasingly matters of considerable concern to everyone who has an interest in the continuance of wildfowling as a sport. The old WAGBI was very keen to foster responsible attitudes amongst sportsmen and, to some extent, this has been continued by the BASC in the form of Codes of Practice. Despite the lead from the fowlers' own organisation, however, there are still too many 'marsh cowboys' who seriously endanger the reputation and future of the craft. In a world where there are many people who seek to have all country sports abolished, it is vital to ensure that our conduct is beyond reproach and not to provide our opponents with ammunition to further their cause.

In any event wildfowling is an activity which impinges upon the world of nature and, as with all such activities, there is placed upon the fowler an overriding responsibility for the welfare of the birds and beasts of the countryside. The wildfowler harvests part of the annual surplus of duck and geese; at no time should his activities be permitted to contribute to a depletion of the ongoing population of any species.

Respect is a word which has already cropped up several times in the preceding pages and it is a concept which is absolutely fundamental to our sport. Respect for both the wildfowl we pursue and respect for our fellow men are the bases of the universally accepted rules of the game.

The Wildfowler's Ten Commandments

1. Never raise a gun to any bird which cannot be positively identified as a legitimate quarry species.
2. Never shoot at a duck or goose which will not subsequently be enjoyed at the table.
3. Never shoot at any bird which is beyond the range of either gun or marksmanship.
4. Never shoot at a bird which may fall in a place from which it cannot be retrieved.
5. Do not discharge a shotgun within 400 yards of an occupied house before dawn or after dusk.
6. When arriving for morning flight do not disturb anyone who may be asleep.
7. Always arrive with time to spare so as to avoid disturbing the marsh after the flight has begun.
8. On no account take up a position in front of another fowler or within 150 yards to his side.
9. Do not leave your position until the flight is over.
10. If a goose flight is expected, do not disturb the marsh by shooting at duck.

In the days of Colonel Hawker such edicts were perhaps unnecessary because fowlers were born and apprenticed on the shore and their numbers, being small, permitted a large area of saltings to be the exclusive territory of a single Gun. It is probable, too, that a person such as the redoubtable Colonel would not have thought twice about proffering physical violence to anyone foolish enough to disturb a flight on 'his' marsh.

Conduct and Ethics

To the man who obtains his sport at the formal covert shoot it may seem strange that wildfowlers adhere, in the main, to a code of conduct which causes them to let many chances pass them by. Only a person who has experienced at first hand the magic of a dawning estuary can understand that the size of the bag is unimportant to a true fowler. It is enough simply to be there when the fowl flight.

To the law of the land and the accepted ethics of the sport one must add a further moral constraint. Wildfowling, by its very nature, is a foul weather activity and many would maintain that it is hardly worth rising from bed unless there has been a hard frost and gale force winds are howling down the estuary. After a prolonged spell of really hard weather, however, there comes a point at which the guns must be left at home. When inland waters have been frozen for weeks and deep snow covers the fields, duck and geese experience a desperate fight for survival. In this state they provide neither worthwhile sport nor a decent meal and no responsible wildfowler would harry them in such a condition. Indeed, as mentioned previously, the Secretary of State has powers under the *Wildlife and Countryside Act 1981* to order a temporary ban on shooting if his advisers consider that the weather warrants such a move. Before such a stage is reached it is likely that many wildfowling clubs will have called for voluntary restraint.

Those who would denigrate our sport and seek to ban all shooting are expert at latching on to any lapse of ethics or instance of misbehaviour. It behoves each and every one of us, therefore, to set an example of conduct on the saltings which is beyond reproach. If that sounds like rather a pious sermon, let us remember that wildfowling has a long and noble past and that only today's exponents of the art can ensure that it has an equally long and fruitful future.

The controls and regulations which govern wildfowling today are anathema to the few surviving ancients who still carry their heavy fowling pieces down to the saltings. It is indeed a pity that such worthies should be pressed by the march of time and one can readily appreciate the distaste with which they witness the invasion of their foreshores by people from the towns and cities. As the last of that breed pass from the scene, however, the modern wildfowlers who take their place must be ready to accept that a free-for-all on the marsh today would lead to the total demise of the sport as we know it. It is to protect the wildness of our estuarine waters and the well-being of the fowl themselves that we must adhere to codes of practice and observe the statutes and bye-laws of the land. Paradoxically, control is necessary to preserve the freedoms of our sport and he who would flout the regulations and breach the ethics is the greatest danger to those freedoms.

It is tempting to yearn for the days of Hawker and Millais, to hark back to the years when the fenman and his marsh rail could find solitude amongst the bitterns in the sedge jungles of Norfolk or Cambridgeshire. What we must constantly bear in mind is that only a tiny proportion of today's wildfowlers would have found access to any sport at all in those far off times. In many ways we are better able to enjoy our countryside pursuits today than were our forefathers.

A Typical Outing

Lest the novice fowler fears that the picture I have painted is one of hopelessness and gloom, and is tempted to advertise his newly acquired shotgun in the 'For Sale' columns of his local newspaper, let me take the reader out for a morning to an estuary where Millais almost lost his punt and his life in February 1888. Today the river still follows the same course and, although duck may appear to frequent the estuary in fewer numbers than Millais reported, the wildfowl populations have followed an upward trend since a local nature reserve became effective in 1984, and we should have a chance of some sporting shooting.

To arrive in ample time for morning flight we must rise before 4 o'clock and fill the car with our gear. Driving through the market town in the centre of the county, it is gratifying to note that others are up and about. A milk float has already commenced its round and a light glows in the baker's backshop. Eastwards out of the town we travel, through a couple of villages where nothing moves under the street lamps, and on towards the arc lights of the airfield which now borders the north shore of the inner basin. Skirting around the Royal Air Force billets, a jolt from the car tells us that we have crossed the railway lines a trifle too fast.

Leaving Britain's defences to look after themselves for a while, I turn down a side road and point out with a measure of selfish satisfaction that no other tyre marks show in the glistening covering of hoar-frost on the track. Through the forestry we go, stopping only to unlock a combination padlock on one of the gates which gives us access to the sand dunes above the estuary. The first grey streaks of dawn appear in the eastern sky as we march the half-mile through the dunes, both dogs running off their surplus energy as they follow fresh rabbit scents in the coarse grass. A row of concrete tank traps rises from the sand to greet us and I utter a word of caution about the rusty barbed wire which remains in places. It is over 40 years since Hitler's war ended but, still, there are visible — and tangible — reminders of the threat of enemy invasion. Standing beside one of the ugly concrete blocks we listen for a while as the players tune up for a pre-dawn symphony. Redshank and dunlin take the woodwind parts and the roll of breakers far out in the North Sea provides rhythm for the piece.

As we take up our respective positions in the reeds around the 'Goose Pool', a pack of wigeon flights past but, although identified by the whistling of the cocks, they cannot be seen against the inky blackness of the clear overhead sky. Out on the sandflats a mallard utters a single quack and, as if on cue, the music of preening pinkfeet rolls over the shore from their roost at the tide's edge. At least we know that they are there this morning. In the strengthening light a vast panorama unfolds before our eyes. From the low positions of our hides it appears that the horizon is lost in the meeting of sand and sea and sky. Along that indistinct line a group of duck move. Scaup or goldeneye, probably, although at that distance it is not possible to identify the species positively.

Almost unnoticed, the sky has turned golden and the sensation of being alone in a vast wilderness is overpowering. Gulls are moving now, and an occasional crow caws rudely as it leaves the forest and soars down to scavenge amongst the wrack and driftwood along high water mark. Out on the flats the pinks have become silent again and there is an air of expectancy which pervades the whole estuary. The experience can be very little different from that which Millais and his puntsman would have felt a hundred years ago.

Geese flight inland to feed.

Then, as if by a signal from the conductor's baton, the climax of the symphony occurs as 600 pinkfooted geese rise from the sands. The clamour of their calling subsides into a regular melody as the huge flock sorts itself out into orderly skeins, each of which banks steeply and heads inland. This morning I have picked the wrong spot and I can only watch happily as, from a position two hundred yards to my east, you succeed in bringing down the very end bird of the nearest skein. Just being there is worth the journey. The sight and sound of a large flock of wild geese, the communion with nature shared by man and dog, together but alone in a primitive world. The pink which you proudly hold aloft as I come to congratulate you is a bonus.

As we walk slowly back towards the car a blast from the hooter at the papermill calls the workmen from their homes for another day's duty. Passing the perimeter wire of the airfield we can see a jet fighter warming up on the runway, straining against its wheel brakes as the pilot pulls back on the throttle. Shortly, the plane will roar over the roost where the pinkfeet were resting an hour earlier. In the village the dayshift is arriving at the factory and a school bus waits in the square. We are back in the civilised world of the twentieth century.

4

The Natural History
of Wildfowl

One of the principal factors which makes wildfowling a complete country
activity, rather than merely a simple shooting sport, is the opportunity —
indeed the necessity — of understanding fully the habits and habitat of
each of the quarry species. Whereas the gentleman standing at a peg on a
formal covert shoot need not concern himself with the intricacies of
pheasant production, every fowler must become thoroughly steeped in the
natural history of wildfowl if he is ever to successfully come to terms with
the duck and geese of the marsh. That some of the country's most eminent
bird photographers, artists and naturalists are also wildfowlers is no
coincidence. All those activities share a common basis of knowledge and
each is enhanced by that fascinating blend of love, respect and sympathy
for the fowl themselves.

It is by design rather than accident that this chapter appears before those
dealing with guns, clothing, equipment or marshcraft. The greenhorn who
merely seeks targets at which to test his skills with a shotgun would be well
advised to consider clay pigeon shooting rather than wildfowling. In our
sport, discharging the fowling piece is the final, and sometimes infrequent,
act in a lengthy sequence of events and considerations. Our initial priority
is to get to know something of the form and behaviour of the birds which
will become our quarry. By doing so, we shall not only increase our
awareness of the factors which will enable us to become efficient hunters;
we shall also come to appreciate the underlying reasons why we must
observe a strict code of ethics in our relationship with the fowl.

The Wildfowl Family

The taxonomy of the animal kingdom is an absorbing study in its own right
but there is insufficient space in this volume to do justice to the subject.
Suffice it to note at this stage that all the duck and geese which are hunted
by the wildfowler belong to the family *Anatidae* which is then divided into a
number of subfamilies, each of which contains one or more tribes. A
simple classification can be set out as follows:

Class	: *AVES* (birds)
Order	: *ANSERIFORMES*
Family	: *ANATIDAE* (swans, geese and duck)

Subfamily	: *ANSERINAE*		Subfamily	: *ANATINAE*	
Tribe	: *Anserini* — swans		Tribe	: *Tadornini*	— shelduck
	and geese		Tribe	: *Anatini*	— dabbling duck
			Tribe	: *Aythini*	— diving duck
			Tribe	: *Mergini*	— sea duck and
					sawbills

The above tabulation omits the subfamilies and tribes which are not represented in the normal British wildfowl population. Below the level of tribe, the divisions are genera and species so that, for example, the bird which is commonly known as the pintail is the species *Anas acuta* while the teal, also belonging to the genus *Anas*, carries the specific name *Anas crecca*. It is perhaps interesting to note that most of the fowl which the wildfowler would consider to be worthwhile quarry — that is they may be legitimately shot and are good to eat — belong to just four genera of the forty-one which occur within the family *Anatidae*. Two genera of geese, *Anser* (grey geese) and *Branta* (black geese), and two genera of duck, *Anas* and *Aythya*, contain almost every species to which the British fowler will raise his gun.

Those birds which comprise the family *Anatidae* have a large number of common characteristics which help to distinguish them from other groups of birds. Most have webbed feet and all have short legs and long necks. Their flight pattern is typically one of strong continuous wing beats with the outstretched neck being a standard feature. In the next chapter, when considering the question of identifying individual species, we shall see that small variations from those themes help us to differentiate one duck or goose from the next.

Plumage

An unusual but fundamental feature of wildfowl is that, while most birds undergo a gradual moult in which the flight feathers are replaced one or two at a time, the swans, duck and geese shed all their wing feathers simultaneously and hence become flightless for a few weeks. During this moult the birds are protected from predators by a number of mechanisms. Many adult male duck, for instance, moult out of their colourful breeding plumage and, during the flightless period, they are camouflaged in an eclipse plumage which is drab like the females of their species. Others, such as the shelduck, undertake moult migrations to safer areas like the Heligoland sandbanks and do their moulting in conditions of comparative sanctuary.

The plumage characteristics of wildfowl generally can be considered as falling into two distinct groups; those in which the sexes are similar and those in which the males and females have different colourings. The sexing of geese, for instance, is virtually impossible without close examination of the cloacal region. Shelduck too have basically unisex dress throughout the year, with only minor differences evident between male and female. Most species of duck, on the other hand, demonstrate marked sexual dimorphism with the differences being greatest in the dabbling duck. The males of species such as mallard, teal and shoveler are brightly coloured with considerable iridescence, while the females are drab, in feathers of mottled and spotted browns. The diving duck species show similar dimorphism, although the males tend to be less brightly coloured, while in many of the sea duck black and white are the predominant male colours, with their females being somewhat duller. Most of the duck which the wildfowler will encounter can be rather confusing very early in the season when the males may not be fully out of their eclipse plumage and birds of the year will still be in their juvenile garb. The apparent preponderance of females in the fowler's bag during September and early October consequently bears closer examination. It is, incidentally, well worth maintaining a log of all wildfowl shot, showing not only species but also sex and whether juvenile or adult. Studies of sex ratios and relative numbers of young and old birds in the fowler's bag can tell us a lot about species distribution and breeding success.

Frequenting an aquatic environment offers both benefits and problems to wildfowl. As it provides a degree of protection from predation and a fairly rich food supply, a wetland habitat is splendid during the warmer months of the year. The same water, on the other hand, may become most inhospitable in winter when storms or freezing temperatures are the order of the day. To combat the potential discomfort of feeding or roosting in icy water, wildfowl have evolved a covering of fluffy down beneath their outer coats of close-set feathers. The insulating property of duck down has been known for centuries to the manufacturers of bed quilts, and it is significant that even in this age of high technology the most efficient duvets are filled with the natural product, while those utilising artificial materials are often regarded as second-best.

A regular behaviour characteristic of swans, geese and duck is the frequent preening which serves to ensure that the feather fibres retain their interlock and thus maintain the essential element of waterproofing. Additionally, a gland at the base of the bird's tail secretes oil which is spread through the outer feathers during the preening activity and further enhances their weatherproofing properties. Additional protection against the cold is provided by a layer of subcutaneous fat which, in wildfowl in good condition, is substantially thicker than is found in other families of birds.

Feeding

The degree to which wildfowl species are adapted to their environment becomes very clear when we examine their feeding behaviour. Any species will be most successful if it can develop, through the evolutionary process, an exclusive niche which avoids undue competition for food and this state is often attained by the development of specific behavioural or physical characteristics. Diving duck, for instance, tend to have short legs set well back towards the rear of their bodies. This configuration helps them to swim efficiently to gather their food although it causes them to have an ungainly waddle when walking on land. Geese and wigeon, in contrast, are grazing birds and have strong, centrally placed legs which enable them to walk well. Diving duck also have a smaller number of air spaces in their skulls than do the dabbling duck; a feature which allows them to dive with ease to greater depths.

The different depths at which duck feed is an important factor in allowing several species to co-exist without competition for limited food. For example, wigeon graze on land or right at the edge of shallow water; teal, mallard and pintail frequently feed by 'upending' in fairly shallow water but can reach different depths because of the relative lengths of their necks; pochard and tufted duck can dive to a depth of many feet.

Variations in the shape and size of the bill similarly reflect differing diets. The broad-billed dabbling duck sieve water and mud to find the small crustaceans and vegetable particles upon which they feed, with the handsome shoveler exhibiting an archetypal example of this adaptation. Grazing duck and geese, on the other hand, have shorter, more pointed bills, while the fish-eating mergansers are endowed with serrated bills which enable them to grip their slithery prey.

In addition to physical differences, wildfowl have also evolved a number of behaviour patterns which reflect their feeding requirements. Many species, especially in winter, engage in flock feeding and some, such as the shoveler, appear to unconsciously co-operate by feeding in long lines so that one bird can sieve the water which has been disturbed by the feet of the duck in front.

Migration

There can be little doubt that one of the principal reasons for man's fascination with wildfowl is the wonder and awe which their migratory behaviour engenders. We may feel more than a tinge of sadness when the great skeins of grey geese leave our shores each springtime but we are sustained through the summer months by the certain knowledge that their evocative music will again gladden our hearts when they return in the autumn.

Journeys of several thousand miles are not uncommon, and yet birds carrying identification rings are known to return to the same locations year after year. The precise mechanism by which migration is guided is not fully understood and is probably not identical throughout all species of migratory birds. Swallows, for example, have a very highly developed sense of direction and naïve young birds will find their way to breeding or feeding grounds without the benefit of previous experience or adult company. At this level there appears to be a high degree of instinct involved, similar to that of a homing pigeon which can be taken hundreds of miles in a closed basket and, upon release, will quickly orientate itself and head home to its loft.

In contrast, it seems likely that memory and experiential learning are of greater importance in the migration patterns of wildfowl. Whereas there may be a certain amount of innate behaviour involved in the timing of migrations and in navigating over sea areas, duck and geese have a greater ability to alter their patterns of movement in response to environmental changes than do some of the smaller migrant birds. That geese remain in family groups, the eldest of which may have undertaken several migration cycles, is clearly an advantage in finding areas in which food was plentiful in previous years. Unlike some other birds, geese which are reared in captivity will not necessarily find their way to suitable breeding grounds unless they join up with a wild flock.

The general scheme of wildfowl migration is north-south, with birds in the northern hemisphere spending the winter in a more southerly location than that in which they will breed. Of all the true migratory wildfowl which grace our shores, only the garganey breeds and summers here before travelling south to spend winter in Africa. All others have their principal breeding grounds close to the Arctic Circle and undertake an autumn migration to reside with us during the winter months. In addition to the true migrants, the complete populations of which move in spring and autumn, a relatively large number of duck species are partial migrants to Britain. In these cases, of which the mallard and teal are prime examples, there is a resident British breeding stock which is supplemented by an overwintering population from more northern climes. An unusual case is that of the shoveler. It is thought that all shoveler do migrate despite giving the appearance of residing in Britain throughout the year. Ringing studies appear to suggest that those individuals which breed in the UK travel to southern Europe in autumn, to be replaced by others which have bred in Scandinavia and the USSR.

The distance travelled by migrating fowl can vary from a few hundred miles to several thousand. Frequently, it is the smaller species which make the longest journeys. Pinkfooted geese migrating from Iceland to Scotland do so in a single journey and typically travel the 800 miles in less than twenty-four hours. At a mean height of 2,000 feet and with an air speed of up to forty miles per hour, they probably use the sun and stars to navigate over the north Atlantic, although in adverse weather conditions they can be blown a considerable distance off their normal routes. At the other end of the scale duck such as wigeon, pintail and goldeneye may travel almost

2,000 miles from their breeding grounds in the central Soviet Union and do so in stages over a period of several weeks.

In addition to the chief north-south autumn and spring migration pattern, which is a relatively common phenomenon in the avian world, there are two other pseudo-migrations which may be encountered in several wildfowl species. As mentioned earlier, a number of duck species seek protection during the flightless period by undertaking a moult migration to areas of comparative safety before shedding their flight feathers. One inland water in Germany regularly accommodates a moulting flock of over 10,000 pochard, while up to 250,000 sea duck moult in the shallow waters of the sea around Denmark. In Britain, it is known that non-breeding Canada geese from the Yorkshire population migrate to the Beauly Firth in northern Scotland to moult, leaving the breeding pairs on their home territory.

Large scale movements of duck can also be occasioned by hard weather, as instanced by the increased numbers of teal, wigeon and mallard which may be counted in eastern Britain when a prolonged, severe freeze-up affects the Netherlands and northern Germany.

Breeding

The breeding habits of wildfowl can form a fascinating study in their own right and several of the natural history books listed in Appendix A will provide a great deal of detailed information.

Most species of swans, geese and duck are noted for their distinctive courtship displays which serve to form pair bonds between male and female and also help to prevent hybridisation between closely related species. In general terms the displays accentuate prominent plumage characteristics and frequently involve exaggerated neck and head movements and a variety of vocal signals. It is interesting to note, however, that whereas geese typically remain with a chosen mate for several seasons, the duck species tend to be rather more flirty and it is normal for drakes to take no part in protecting the nest or rearing the ducklings.

Because they usually nest at ground level, the nests of duck are subject to fairly high losses as a result of predation and flooding. Foxes and feral mink will take a sitting duck and her eggs, while gulls, skuas and even pike are a constant threat to young ducklings. While fishing on Loch Leven one evening in early summer I watched impotently as a pair of black-backed gulls picked off an entire brood of nine mallard ducklings. The mother duck attempted in vain to defend her offspring but the ducklings, which could not have been more than three of four days old, had no chance and were gulped down whole by the gulls.

Geese have a smaller brood than most duck species but suffer rather less from predation on account of their larger size and the fact that both parents share the task of guarding the nest and the goslings.

The level of fertility of wildfowl eggs is high and if incubation is not interrupted more than ninety per cent will normally hatch. All duck and geese are nidifugous, that is to say that the chicks can walk and swim within a few hours of hatching. They do, however, require the body heat of their mother to prevent chilling and they also obtain a coating of waterproofing oil from the duck's plumage which enables their own down to repel water and retain warmth. Ducklings which are hatched in an incubator and brooded artificially will chill and die if they get soaked during the first couple of weeks of their life.

Young wildfowl grow very rapidly and those which breed in Arctic areas are required to be fully fledged and ready to undertake an arduous migration by the end of the short northern summer. The timing of the breeding cycle is clearly important and there is evidence to suggest that day-length is the critical factor which triggers the behaviour sequence so as to result in the chicks hatching at a time of optimum food availability. Some wildfowl collectors have experienced difficulty in successfully breeding a few of the species which normally summer in the high Arctic and it may be that this problem results from the shorter day-length which we have in Britain during the normal breeding season.

After the young birds are fully fledged, the majority of wildfowl species are relatively secure from serious predation. While the diminutive teal may fall prey to a roving raptor, most duck and geese have few natural enemies other than man and the ubiquitous fox. Despite ringing studies regularly turning up geese and duck which have lived for ten years or more, it remains a fact that over fifty per cent of some species will have been killed by the end of their second year. In the case of species which are sought as quarry by wildfowlers death is most commonly by shooting, although a study of population dynamics confirms that, were this not so, losses from starvation, exhaustion and disease would take an increased toll.

Population Dynamics

The population of any species is affected by recruitment and mortality; that is, additions to the population arising from the production of young and removals from it due to death. If the levels of recuitment and mortality do not balance, then the population will either increase or decline. Probably the most important concept to be developed by scientists studying population dynamics is that of density dependent compensation. Many factors such as the number of nesting sites and the availability of food will have an effect on the overall population level of a wildfowl species, either by influencing breeding success or death rate.

The important result of those findings, from the point of view of the wildfowler, is that up to a finite threshold level the harvesting of duck and geese by shooting will not cause a reduction in the overall population. There must, of course, be a limit to the degree of shooting losses which can be made up by compensatory factors and more research will be required before positive species management, of the type practised in the USA, can be confidently introduced to Britain. Indeed, given the responsible attitudes to shooting which are being encouraged by the BASC, it may well be the case that regulations and bag limits of the American type will never be required in this country. Certainly, at the present time, many of the quarry species are experiencing an upward population trend in Britain.

Importance to Wildfowlers

An understanding of the natural history of duck and geese is important to wildfowlers for a number of reasons. In the main, wildfowl are flighted when they are travelling between roost and feeding grounds. The fowler must choose his position with care and take into account the feeding patterns of the species which he hopes to encounter. Decoying and calling take advantage of the flock-feeding characteristics of some species and, in such cases, the wildfowler must know the behaviour patterns of the birds.

The effects which weather, wind and tides have upon the fowl must also be understood. To a very large extent, successful wildfowling depends upon being in the right place at the right time and this is an art which can only be perfected with the benefit of a great deal of both knowledge and experience.

Wildfowling is concerned with taking part of the annual harvestable surplus of the goose and duck populations and it is inherent in this concept that the fowler must strive to ensure that the well-being of his quarry is promoted. Later in this book we shall look in detail at some of the practical conservation measures which can, and have been, taken by wildfowling clubs. In the meantime it is worth repeating that it behoves every apprentice fowler to study his quarry in order that he might fully appreciate the behaviour of geese and ducks and understand the population dynamics which must be kept in balance if the future of his sport is to be safeguarded.

5
Wildfowl of the Marshes

In Britain we are particularly fortunate to have such a wide range of wildfowl species frequenting our estuaries, marshes and inland waters. From the point of view of the wildfowler this wealth of birdlife adds interest to every outing but it also places upon the sportsman a heavy responsibility to be able to identify each of the species and to differentiate those which may legally be shot from those which are protected.

Many years ago, when the shooting list was considerably longer than it is today, I regularly met a real old-time fowler on my trips to the local estuary. Bert MacPhee was one of those characters about whom a book should have been written or a film made but, as is so often the case, he was dead and buried before anyone thought about recording his personal reminiscences for posterity. With his damascus-barrelled hammer gun and home-loaded black powder cartridges he culled a considerable harvest from the muddy foreshores of eastern Scotland and he would readily impart the benefit of his accumulated wisdom and homespun advice in return for a few glasses of malt whisky. Whether the advice was worth the price might have been debatable but the manner in which it was delivered, and the stories which accompanied it, made a few hours in the public bar a sound investment.

Although Bert had received virtually no formal education and had scant regard for matters such as proof regulations, personal safety or sporting etiquette, he possessed a finely-tuned ability to understand the world of nature within which he hunted. He also demonstrated an almost uncanny knack for correctly identifying birds which were barely visible to the naked eye. On many murky dawns I crouched beside him in a muddy gully and marvelled as he pointed out duck almost a mile down the river channel and decreed them to be scaup, goldeneye, mallard or wigeon. If the birds came in the right direction and presented the chance of a shot, Bert was inevitably proved to be correct in his recognition. When asked how he could identify fowl which were too far distant to provide any clues of colour or shape, his answer was merely, 'It's the way they fly, laddie.'

And indeed it is. The wildfowler cannot rely upon the nice colour plates in a birdwatcher's field guide to help him decide whether to pull the trigger or lower his gun. Whereas Bert MacPhee would have been unable to describe the mental process by which he recognised the flight characteristics

A skein of pinkfooted geese.

of each species, it is possible with careful analysis to break down the factors such as flight speed, wingbeat, wing-to-body ratio and flight aspect which allow the fowler to differentiate one species from another in the conditions which prevail on a dawning estuary.

Duck and Geese of the Shore

Traditionally the principal quarry of the coastal wildfowler has comprised wigeon, mallard, teal and the grey geese, but others such as pintail, shoveler, pochard and tufted duck are welcome additions to the bag in many areas. For the purposes of describing the duck and geese of the shore, it may be useful to give most attention to those species which are either common quarry or, conversely, are protected species which the fowler may frequently encounter. For the sake of completeness, descriptions of the sea-duck and sawbills is included but information regarding status and habits is provided in greater detail for the species which are of particular importance to the longshore gunner.

Mallard *(Anas platyrhynchos)*

Undoubtedly the mallard must be the best known of all duck in the British

Wildfowl silhouettes.

Isles. Apart from being common in city parks and canals, it is also the standard duck of children's books, calendars and greetings cards.

Appearance

The head and neck of the male are iridescent bottle green and are separated from the chestnut breast by a narrow white neck-ring. The underbody and wing coverts are predominantly grey with the characteristic blue-purple, white-edged speculum being a striking feature. Tail coverts are black with the four central feathers upturned. A greenish-yellow bill and orange legs complete the familiar picture. The female is a much less colourful bird of mottled brown and paler underparts. Her bill is orange and the legs are somewhat weaker in colour than those of the drake but the iridescent speculum is shared by both sexes. Juveniles and the male in eclipse plumage are essentially similar in appearance to the female.

Status and Habits

In Europe the mallard breeds from the Mediterranean to north of the Arctic Circle. Birds pair as soon as the drakes show breeding plumage in late autumn, their courtship displays normally taking place on water. Between nine and thirteen eggs are laid in a nest and incubation does not begin until the clutch is complete. After twenty-eight days the ducklings hatch out covered in fluffy down and before long they will be swimming behind their mother, picking insects off the water surface. Adult mallard feed principally on vegetable matter and, although the standard method of feeding is dabbling in shallow water, they take a certain amount of grain and potatoes in autumn in agricultural areas.

As the most numerous duck in Europe, the mallard population shows no evidence of decline, possibly due to the great adaptability of the species to changes in the environment. The number of breeding pairs in Britain has increased considerably in recent years and is now thought to number over 100,000 pairs. When migrant visitors and released birds are taken into account, the overwintering population is in excess of 350,000 birds and may, in peak months, approach half a million. Mortality is, however, very high, being estimated at an average annual loss of sixty-five per cent of the population.

Many a gourmet would claim a corn-fed wild mallard in September to be the ultimate culinary delight obtainable from the wildfowl world. It would be very difficult to contradict such a statement when the mind conjures up pictures of duck basted in honey and served with orange sauce. As a quarry species the bird is both challenging and sporting provided, of course, that it is hunted in truly wild conditions.

Wigeon *(Anas penelope)*

Many wildfowlers would suggest that the wigeon is *the* duck of the estuary, and there can be little doubt that a pack flighting overhead, their characteristic whistle shrilling from a dark sky, is guaranteed to set the blood racing through the veins of a seasoned marsh gunner. Somewhat smaller than a mallard, the wigeon is another bird which can provide supremely sporting shooting. Its culinary qualities are hotly debated amongst fowlers, some claiming that it rivals the mallard, while others consider that special recipes and sauces are required to render it palatable. To a large extent, the acceptability of the flavour of wigeon flesh probably depends upon what the bird has been feeding on and it is certainly a better table bird early in the season.

Appearance

The male in breeding plumage has a chestnut head with a pale yellow forehead and crown, a pinkish-grey breast and mainly grey back and sides. The white forewing coverts show up boldly in flight, as do the very light underparts. The female and juvenile are predominantly rusty brown mottled with dark chestnut and they share the lighter belly of the male. Both sexes have a dark green speculum which is somewhat less prominent than that of most species of dabbling duck. In eclipse the male takes on the general coloration of the female but retains his white shoulder patches. The short pointed bill is typically grey with a dark tip and the legs are dark grey or black.

Status and Habits

Only small numbers of wigeon breed in Britain, mainly in Scotland and north-west England, the principal breeding grounds being in the Soviet Union, Scandinavia and Iceland. The nest is invariably at ground level and the female has sole responsibility for incubating the eight or nine eggs. Like most of the *Anas* genera, the duckling are led to water as soon as their down has dried. Until 1930 the chief food of wigeon overwintering in Britain was *Zostera*, an eelgrass found on mudbanks. An epidemic of virus disease destroyed much of this grass, however, and since then wigeon have become much more catholic in their feeding habits, taking cereals, root crops and sprouting winter wheat, in addition to marsh grasses and algae. There are recent signs that *Zostera* might be poised to make a comeback on some coastlines and, provided that pollution can be controlled, wildfowlers may witness a gradual reversion to the traditional habits and haunts of wigeon.

Up to 250,000 wigeon winter in Britain, the main sites being the Cromarty Firth, Lindisfarne, the Ouse Washes and the Medway, Swale and Thames estuaries. There is some current concern that the distribution of wigeon within the British Isles is changing, with the populations of certain east coast sites being diminished in favour of the west. Research indicates a disproportionately high incidence of adult males in the overwintering population, suggesting that differential migration patterns exist for this species.

Teal *(Anas crecca)*

Appearance

The European green-winged teal is the smallest duck on the wildfowler's shooting list but the male in full plumage makes up for his diminutive size by his striking good looks. The glossy chestnut head has an iridescent curving green stripe, with narrow cream edging, running from the eye to the back of the neck. The striated body plumage is well known to anglers who dress their own trout and salmon flies and there is a white horizontal stripe above the wing. A prominent green speculum is present in both sexes. The female, juvenile and male in eclipse plumage are very similar with their mottled browns and paler belly. The legs and bill of both sexes are dark grey, tinged with brown.

Status and Habits

The teal breeds sparsely throughout Britain but the main summer haunts are in the northern Soviet Union, Scandinavia and Iceland. Up to 90,000 birds regularly migrate to Britain from those areas for the winter and the numbers may be temporarily swollen if extremely hard weather affects the Netherlands. In many respects, such as breeding and feeding habits, teal are very similar to mallard in their behaviour. Indeed, the two species may frequently be found feeding and roosting in close proximity.

Despite their small size, teal are very good to eat and, being fairly timid by nature, they are by no means an easy quarry for the sportsman. The clay pigeon term 'springing teal' derives from the tendency of the little duck to engage in vertical take-off manoeuvres when it is disturbed.

Garganey *(Anas querquedula)* (Protected)

The little garganey is the only duck which is exclusively a summer visitor to Britain, breeding sparsely in southern England and migrating to tropical Africa for the winter.

Appearance

Slightly larger than the teal, the male in full plumage has a brown head and breast with a sickle-shaped white band from above the eye to the nape of the neck. The body is mottled grey-brown with paler sides and black-edged white scapular feathers. The female, juvenile and male in eclipse are largely grey-brown with darker mottling on the wings. In both sexes the speculum is pale green and cream.

Status and Habits

In many respects the natural history of garganey is similar to that of the teal although, in fact, it is more closely related to the shoveler or the American blue-winged teal. Since 1981 it has been protected by law, although prior to that date very few wildfowlers would have deliberately killed a garganey as the total number breeding in the British Isles probably does not exceed 100 pairs. Because they leave their haunts in this country in September they are not often encountered by fowlers but to mistake the female for an early season teal is an understandable error.

Pintail *(Anas acuta)*

Appearance

The handsome pintail must be a strong contender for the distinction of being Europe's most elegant wildfowl species. In breeding plumage the male is resplendent in chocolate head and neck with a white stripe extending upwards from breast to ear. Grey upperparts and flanks are set off by beautiful lanceolated scapulars of black, yellow and grey and there is a pale yellow patch in front of the distinctive black tail coverts. The long 'pin' tail is the identifier which, of course, gives the bird its popular name. The female shares the slender neck and body of the male but is generally a light mottled chestnut with paler underparts. Juveniles are similar to the female but males in eclipse are somewhat greyer and may be distinguished by the bronze-green speculum on the wing. Bill and legs are grey with a bluish tinge.

Status and Habits

The winter diet of the pintail is similar to that of the mallard and the upending posture is common when feeding in water. In their breeding grounds, however, more animal matter is consumed, principally in the form of midge and caddis-fly larvae. A few pintail breed in eastern Britain but the main concentrations are to be found in the 'duck factory' of the central and northern regions of the Soviet Union. In winter a variable population of up to 25,000 birds may come to this country, concentrating on the Dee and Mersey estuaries, although smaller numbers will be found in most coastal areas and some inland waters.

In those areas where it is relatively plentiful the pintail is regarded as a fine wildfowling quarry and, provided it has not been feeding exclusively on the saltmarsh, it is a good table bird.

Shoveler *(Anas clypeata)*

Appearance

A very distinctive bird, the shoveler displays the ultimate in dabbling equipment — a very broad spatulate bill which gives an immediate clue to the species' feeding habits. The drake in breeding dress has a bottle-green head, white neck and chest, dark chestnut flanks and underparts and dark brownish-grey wing coverts. The colouring of the female is similar to that of other dabbling duck but the shovel bill makes misidentification unlikely. Both sexes have a green speculum and display a blue-grey patch on the forewing, similar to that of the garganey and American blue-winged teal.

Status and Habits

About 1,000 pairs breed in Britain, primarily in the east, the nest being built close to water and typically nine to eleven eggs being laid. The male is more territorial than other dabbling duck species and will defend the area around the nest while the female is incubating the eggs. The newly hatched ducklings have tiny shovel bills which immediately distinguish them from the young of other species. Unlike most duck which both breed and winter in Britain, shoveler are totally migratory, the entire breeding stock leaving in autumn for France, Spain and Africa and being replaced by an over-wintering population of up to 9,000 birds which have bred in Scandinavia and the Soviet Union.

Because the winter stock is distributed widely throughout the country, they are not likely to turn up in large numbers in the wildfowler's bag and, when they do, they will probably not be enjoyed at the table as much as a good mallard, teal or pintail.

Gadwall *(Anas strepera)*

Appearance

Slightly smaller than the mallard but very similar in build, the gadwall is a relatively uncommon bird in Britain. The drake is predominantly grey with a brown-tinged back. The female is very mallard-like but may be distinguished by the white speculum which it shares with the male. The bill of the female has conspicuous orange edges which, although not present in the drake when in full plumage, are taken on in eclipse.

Status and Habits
Breeding and feeding habits are similar to the mallard although the gadwall requires permanent water before it will nest. During the breeding season both sexes appear to become carnivorous, with invertebrate life comprising a larger portion of the diet rather than at other times of the year.

About 250–300 pairs breed in Britain, mainly in East Anglia and south-east Scotland, and the overwintering population probably approaches 4,000 birds. The principal haunts are central Europe in summer and the Mediterranean regions in winter.

Although gadwall do not feature extensively in the wildfowler's bag, the species is said to be excellent to eat. As a sporting quarry they are somewhat variable and may, at times, be rather lacking in caution. At Loch Leven it is thought that the number of gadwall shot by the official wild-fowling parties is out of proportion to the population because of their vulnerability to shooting.

Tufted Duck (*Aythya fuligula*)

All of the species considered so far have been dabbling duck of the genus *Anas*. In the tufted duck we come to the first member of the diving duck genus *Aythya*, which also contains the pochard and the scaup. The 'tuftie' is very common on most waters in Britain and occurs both as a breeding species and as a winter migrant.

Appearance
When in full breeding regalia the male has a black head, back and tail with pure white flanks. The head is shot with purple while the chest often displays a greenish tinge. The popular name for the duck derives from a drooping black crest which is not normally obvious at a distance but which is, in fact, fairly long. The bill is blue-grey with a black tip, the legs are grey and the eye is bright orange. The female's colouring is less contrasting than the male, her upperparts being dark brown and her flanks pale rust. In eclipse the male resembles the female but usually has lighter flanks. Both female and male in eclipse have a shorter crest than the breeding male.

Status and Habits
Tufted duck normally nest very close to water and typically eight to eleven greenish-grey eggs will be laid. The male participates in guarding the brood which, like most duck species, takes to the water within hours of hatching. On the islands of Loch Leven tufted duck frequently nest in the midst of

colonies of black-headed gulls, thereby effectively reducing predation by hooded crows, jackdaws and black-backed gulls. Tufties feed by diving for molluscs, insect larvae and crustaceans at depths of up to ten feet although they have been known to dive considerably deeper on occasion.

The breeding range extends over much of central and northern Europe, with up to 7,000 pairs throughout Britain. In winter the population in this country swells to 50,000 birds, mainly migrants from Iceland, Scandinavia and the Baltic regions. Both breeding and winter populations have substantially increased in Britain since 1950 and the species is noted for its adaptibility, frequently being one of the first to use new reservoirs and gravel workings.

As a quarry species the tufted duck is not regarded as highly as the mallard, teal or pintail but it can provide sporting shooting at times. On coastal waters great care must be taken to correctly identify the tuftie, as the scaup — which is not dissimilar in appearance — is now a protected species. The flesh of tufties which have been feeding on estuaries tends not to be particularly sought-after for culinary purposes, although birds which have been feeding in fresh water can be good to eat.

Pochard *(Aythya ferina)*

Appearance
In full breeding plumage the pochard is a striking bird displaying a red-brown head, black breast and throat and slate-grey back. The bill is blue-grey with a black tip and the legs are dark grey. In eclipse the red eye of the male distinguishes it from the dull brown female.

Status and Habits
Between 200 and 300 pairs breed in the British Isles and the winter population numbers around 45,000 birds. The Thames estuary and reservoirs around London are favoured haunts and Duddingston Loch in Edinburgh once harboured a major winter concentration. This latter population fed on the Forth estuary and, like the scaup, virtually deserted the area when a new treatment plant began to purify the sewage from the city. The major breeding grounds are in the western Soviet Union. In recent years a moulting flock of up to 3,000 birds has gathered annually at Abberton Reservoir in Essex.

The pochard feeds predominantly on water plants for which it dives in water up to ten feet deep. This vegetable diet is probably the reason why the pochard is the most palatable of all the diving duck and, as such, is a worthwhile quarry for the wildfowler. In hard weather, when inland waters have been frozen for several weeks, the pochard tends to feed on estuarine molluscs and crustaceans, and at such times, its culinary value is greatly reduced.

Scaup *(Aythya marila)* (Protected)

Appearance
The scaup is closely related to the tufted duck to which it bears a close resemblance. The breeding male has a black head, shot with green, black breast, light grey wings and white flanks and belly. The female is predominantly brown with paler flanks and underparts.

Status and Habits
The scaup breeds only sparsely in northern Britain but flocks of up to 15,000 birds regularly winter on our shores. At one time the largest concentration was on the Firth of Forth where thousands of scaup congregated around the main sewage outfall from the city of Edinburgh. Measures to reduce environmental pollution led to a new sewage treatment plant being commissioned and, as a result, the huge flocks of scaup moved elsewhere! The northern shores of the Forth still hold important numbers of scaup, and the Eden estuary in Fife and the island of Islay are other favoured winter haunts.

Goldeneye *(Bucephala clangula)*

Appearance
The mature male has an iridescent green head with a prominent white patch between bill and eye. The back is black and the neck and underparts white or light grey. The female has a mainly grey body with a chestnut-brown head. As the name suggests, the eyes are golden and the short bill and sloping forehead give the head a triangular appearance.

Status and Habits
Like several others of the *Mergini* tribe, the goldeneye nests in holes in trees, usually fairly close to water. No nest material is used, the eight to ten blue-green eggs being laid amongst down plucked from the duck. When the ducklings hatch they scramble out of the nest hole, drop to the ground and are led towards water. The principal foods are molluscs, fish fry, some vegetable matter and crustaceans.

Only a few pairs of goldeneye breed in the British Isles, the main summer haunts being the western Soviet Union, Finland and northern Scandinavia. About 12,000 birds overwinter in Britain with large concentrations in the Forth estuary in Scotland and Lough Neagh in Northern Ireland.

Several writers have classified the goldeneye as inedible and, when it has been feeding on the saltmarsh, there is a certain similarity between the flavour of its flesh and that of par-boiled seaweed. If the wildfowler is fortunate to come across a population from an inland water habitat, however, this attractive little duck is well worth cooking.

Shelduck *(Tadorna tadorna)* (Protected)

Appearance

Both sexes have a black head and neck, a white body and a rich brown yoke at shoulder level. There is a dark stripe down the underparts and the wing primaries are black. The male may be distinguished by the knob at the base of its bright red bill.

Status and Habits

The shelduck is present throughout the year in Britain and in some localities its numbers might cause the casual observer to wonder why it requires to be protected by law. Fortunately it is so distinctive in appearance that there is never any excuse for mistaking it for any other bird. Around 10,000 pairs breed in Britain with the nests being made in holes in sand dunes, banks or rocky crevices. Nest sites are sometimes used by more than one female and, although the average clutch size is eleven, up to thirty-two eggs have been recorded in a single nest. Only one female incubates the eggs in communal nests of this type.

In winter there may be up to 60,000 shelduck in Britain, accounting for almost half of the north-west European population. The largest single concentration is on the Wash where more than 14,000 birds have been recorded.

The principal food of shelduck is the tiny saltwater mollusc *Hydrobia ulvae* which is found in the mud of many estuaries and is sometimes present in enormous densities. In very severe weather, when estuarine mud freezes, shelduck experience considerable difficulty in obtaining food and many have been known to die in very hard winters.

Eider *(Somateria mollissima)* (Protected)

Appearance

The male eider in full plumage is predominantly white with a black forehead, crown and underparts. The rear sides of the head have a greenish tinge and there is a pink hue in the breast feathers. The female is brown with dark barring.

Status and Habits

The eider is best known for its down which at one time was extremely popular as a bed quilting. Like the shelduck, the eider is by no means uncommon and the reasons for affording it legal protection are dubious. One consolation, however, is that neither species is likely to be particularly palatable on account of their marine habitat and diet.

The eider is probably the world's most abundant marine duck with the British population numbering about 60,000 birds. The main food is the mussel but other molluscs and many forms of crustaceans and worms are also eaten.

Seaduck and Sawbills (All Protected)

Most of the more common sea duck will occasionally be seen by the coastal wildfowler but all are protected by law and none is likely to be misidentified as a quarry species.

The common scoter *(Melanitta nigra)* male is the only duck to have completely black plumage. It has a grey and orange bill with a dark grey knob at the base. The female is dark rust brown with fawn cheeks. Around 20,000 birds winter around the coasts of Britain, the principal haunt being the Moray Firth.

The velvet scoter *(Melanitta fusca)* is somewhat rarer in Britain than the common scoter and the male velvet scoter may be distinguished by a white spot behind the eye and a white wing patch. The female is brown but lacks the extensive pale cheeks of the common scoter.

The male long-tailed duck *(Clangula hyemalis)* is the only duck to have three plumage phases in its annual cycle. In early summer it is predominantly brown with a white patch on the face and white flanks and underparts. In this phase the characteristic long pointed tail is present. In eclipse it loses its tail and becomes generally duller in coloration. The tail feathers are regrown in winter and the head, scapulars and flanks are white, the eye-surrounds are grey and the ear and breast are brown. By contrast, the female spends the entire year in dull brown with white sides to the neck and head. She also lacks the long tail feathers of the male. Up to 5,000 long-tailed duck winter off the British coasts, mainly in the north and east. The most important breeding grounds of the European population are in the western Soviet Union, Finland, Scandinavia and Iceland.

Two sawbills, the goosander *(Mergus merganser)* and the red-breasted merganser *(Mergus serrator)*, were once classed as vermin in Scotland but since 1981 they have been afforded full protection throughout Britain. The goosander is the larger of the two, but both are unusual in that the males have white and black bodies and green-black heads whereas the bodies of the females are grey and their heads red-brown. The long serrated bills give an immediate clue to the diet of these duck, the major part of which consists of fish.

Greylag Goose *(Anser anser)*

Undoubtedly the great grey geese are the longshore gunner's most prized quarry. There are men who derive great satisfaction from hunting mallard or wigeon or teal but there must be few for whom the excitement is not doubled when straining ears pick up the music of approaching geese.

Appearance

One of the larger grey geese, the greylag is the stock from which most British farmyard geese are descended. Both sexes are brownish grey with paler grey forewings and white barred tail coverts. The large heavy bill is orange in the western race and the legs are flesh-coloured.

Status and Habits

Although a number of greylag nest in the Hebrides, and a few feral flocks are now established in other parts of Britain, the major winter population on our shores comes from Iceland. Around 100,000 birds make the annual migration over the north Atlantic to spend the colder months of the year in east and central Scotland with smaller numbers wintering on the Solway and around Morecambe Bay.

Greylag normally breed in their third year, the nest being built in heather, long grass or raised areas of marsh. Between four and eight creamy white eggs are laid, incubation taking 28–30 days. The male guards the nest and the young, with family groups frequently remaining together until the following season.

In this country the principal foods are grass and cereals, with very little damage being done in economic terms. The greylag is, however, able to adapt its feeding habits rapidly and changing patterns of agricultural land use have resulted in carrots, sugar beet and turnips being consumed. The only time when greylag can be considered a serious agricultural pest is during very wet weather when they will puddle fields and turn newly seeded land into a sea of mud.

Once the wildfowler has become accustomed to the speed and height of these great birds, he will obtain sporting shooting at morning flight as they come off the estuaries on their way to feed in the fields. In common with other grey geese, they should never be shot in the evening on their roosts lest they desert the area completely in search of safer ground. It goes without saying that they are excellent table birds provided that they are in good condition and are not too old. Whereas mallard and teal appear not to become tough-fleshed with age, the same is certainly not true in the case of geese.

Pinkfooted Goose *(Anser brachyrhynchus)*

Without any doubt the pinkfooted goose is my personal favourite from amongst all wildfowl species. Whether painting, photographing or shooting, the form and plumage of the pinkfoot epitomises the majesty of the grey geese. It is without difficulty that my mind travels back to a November morning on the Eden estuary when, within a few hundred yards of the world-famous St Andrews golf course, I shot my very first goose. Since that day I have retained an affection for both the place and the species.

Appearance

Somewhat smaller and daintier than the greylag, the pinkfoot is character-ised by a chocolate-brown head and neck. The body is paler brown with bluish-grey tinges in the wing coverts and darker grey in the tail. The rump, as in all grey geese, is white. The bill of the pinkfoot is smaller and neater than that of the greylag, being pink coloured with variable black markings at base and tip. As the name suggests, the feet and legs are pink.

Status and Habits

The western population of pinkfeet breeds in Iceland and eastern Greenland and the entire population migrates to Britain in autumn. Overwintering numbers are roughly comparable to the greylag population, having risen from 80,000 to over 100,000 in the past decade. Whereas the major wintering ground is again east and central Scotland, the pinkfoot is somewhat more widely dispersed, with significant numbers being found in north-west England, the Solway and north-east Scotland. Regrettably, the once-famous goose grounds around the Wash and East Anglia no longer host the plentiful pinkfoot flocks of yesteryear.

The other major pinkfoot population breeds in Spitzbergen and winters in Denmark, Germany and the Netherlands. It seems likely that the occasional birds sighted in south-east England are vagrants from this population.

The nests of pinkfooted geese may be used year after year, growing a little higher as each season's accumulation of excreta, down and vegetation is added. Four or five off-white eggs are laid and incubated for 26–27 days. The male shares the task of guarding eggs and goslings from predation by gulls, skuas and arctic foxes.

The wintering feeding patterns of pinkfeet are similar to those of greylag, although root crops tend to be less favoured. The exception is the ubiquitous potato stubble which will attract huge flocks of pinkfeet like a magnet. Again, the conflict between farmer and goose is imagined rather than real, the positive benefits of checking potato disease and strengthening the growth of winter wheat and barley probably outweighing any damage done to grazing or early cereal crops. In Perthshire, Fife and Angus the most noise appears to be made by tenant farmers who, by insisting that geese are vermin, are permitted to authorise shooting on their rented fields. They would argue that the large sums of money transferred to their hip pockets from the wallets of visiting goose shooters is merely incidental to the crop protection being obtained.

As a quarry species in truly wild conditions, such as those presented by a gale-whipped estuary, the pinkfooted goose can provide absolutely superb sport. Once again, it is superfluous to extol its merits on the dining table.

Bean Goose *(Anser fabalis)* (Protected)

Appearance

The bean goose is a very large bird with dark brown head and neck and dull brown underparts. The breast is light brown, there are pale edgings to the wing coverts and the bill is orange with black markings. In flight, with no clues to scale, it would be very easy to mistake a bean goose for a large pinkfoot. Prior to 1981, when it was on the shooting list, it was in no danger from wildfowlers as the two main British overwintering flocks were safe from sporting Guns. It is, of course, now fully protected.

Status and Habits

The number of bean geese wintering in Britain appears to have fallen markedly since the beginning of the twentieth century and now only about 200 birds are known to visit this country regularly. One flock is centred on the marshes of the River Yare near Norwich and another regularly spends the winter on the locality of Threave Estate, north of the Solway. Each year, however, additional reports are received of small parties of bean geese being seen in other parts of Britain and vagrants regularly turn up amongst skeins of pinkfeet and a few are sometimes found amongst whitefronted goose flocks.

Habits are largely similar to those of pinkfeet and, indeed, the latter species was once thought to be a sub-species of the bean goose.

Whitefronted Goose *(Anser albifrons)* (Protected in Scotland)

Appearance

The Greenland whitefronted goose is a dark goose, predominantly grey-brown with black traverse bars across the lower breast and belly. Adults have a distinctive white forehead. The bill and legs are light orange. Birds of the European race tend to have an overall lighter plumage and a pink bill. The characteristic barring on the belly and white forehead are again present in both sexes.

Status and Habits

Whitefronts feed mainly on grass, frequently choosing large fields and flooded areas, and will occasionally graze winter cereals. The Greenland race is also known to take the roots of cotton grass from the peat bogs of Ireland and Scotland. Breeding habits are similar to the greylag except that colonial nesting appears to be rare in both races of whitefronts.

There are two distinct races of whitefronted geese in Europe. A population of between 12,000 and 15,000 birds breeds in Greenland and winters at the Wexford Slobs in Eire, the Hebridean island of Islay and throughout western Scotland. In Scotland this race is protected by law. A much larger population of European whitefronts breeds in Siberia and migrates to Germany, the Netherlands, Belgium and France with up to 7,000 birds coming to south-west and southern England. The Wildfowl Trust refuge at Slimbridge is a major winter haunt of the species.

Canada Goose *(Branta canadensis)*

Appearance

In North America there are up to fifteen distinct races of Canada goose identified, but those which exist in Britain are probably descended from one or two of the larger-sized races, possibly including the giant Canada, *Branta canadensis maxima*. The head and neck are black with a white patch circling from cheek to chin. The back is brown and the breast and belly greyish-brown with variable traverse barring.

Status and Habits

The Canada is the only black goose on the general British shooting list and the current population in this country is around 20,000, largely in the Midlands and southern England. In the Lake District and south-west Scotland, where attempts have been made to re-introduce greylag as a breeding species, the Canada goose has caused problems as a result of the dominant mating characteristics of the gander which has led to hybridisation with the greys.

The favoured nesting sites are on islands or boggy areas or moorland, often in sizeable colonies. The non-breeding members of the Yorkshire population have developed an interesting annual moult migration to the Beauly Firth area, leaving the breeding pairs to moult close to the nesting grounds. The principal foods are grass, marsh plants and seeds and some limited damage is undoubtedly done to farm crops, mainly by trampling emerging seedlings.

Although this goose is not universally popular as a sportsman's quarry, it can still provide challenging shooting in areas where it has become truly wild. As a table bird it bears no criticism, young specimens which are not fully grown being particularly good to eat.

Barnacle Goose *(Branta leucopsis)* (Protected)

Appearance

This exceptionally attractive little goose is protected throughout the country although some are shot, under licence, on Islay where crop damage is claimed. Both sexes have a black crown, neck and breast with white cheeks. The back is grey with dark barring and the underparts are off-white.

Status and Habits

Around 20,000 birds breed in Greenland and spend the colder months in western Scotland and around the Irish coasts. The other flock of up to 7,000 birds has its breeding grounds on the islands of the Svalbard archipelago, principally Spitzbergen, and winters on the Solway. Although the limits of the respective wintering ranges are only thirty miles apart, there appears to be no intermixing of the populations.

Their principal foods are marsh grasses, clover and waste root crops.

Brent Goose *(Branta bernicla)* (Protected)

Appearance

There are two distinct sub-species of the brent goose. The light-bellied race breeds in Greenland and Spitzbergen and winters in Ireland and at Lindisfarne, while the dark-bellied Siberian population migrates to the Low Countries and south-east England in winter. Both races have a black head, breast and neck and a dark grey-brown back. There is a light patch on each side of the neck and, as the names suggest, the Atlantic population has a lighter belly than the Siberian race.

Status and Habits

The dark-bellied brent goose has increased dramatically in recent years and a change in habits has taken place with the flocks partially forsaking the saltmarsh and adapting to feeding on agricultural land. There is considerable pressure from wildfowlers to have this race returned to the shooting list as the former decline in the sub-species, which led to its protection, would appear to have been well and truly reversed. As to its edibility one can only guess, but it would be reasonable to expect that specimens feeding on farmland would be palatable. Indeed, in the days when brent and wigeon shared the *zostera* beds of the estuarine saltings, both species were regularly sought by puntgunners, and one must assume that there was a ready market for them.

Wildfowl Identification in Field Conditions

Whereas coloured plates and detailed descriptions may be useful when studying resting fowl through binoculars or considering a shot bird in the hand, the wildfowler is more often faced with the problem of identifying geese and duck in conditions of poor light and when the birds are in flight. Becoming expert at this task can only result from years of experience, during which slight differences in wing beat speed, flashes of dark or light colour, wing-to-body ratios and details of flight sound and calls will, often unconsciously, act as 'keys' to enable positive identification.

To provide a starting point for the novice who is about to take to the shore, I have detailed below some of the more constant 'keys' which help to brand the more common quarry and protected species in that split second before the gun is raised to the shoulder. From such a base each wildfowler must develop his own battery of identifiers to suit the fowl which inhabit his local marsh and, to some extent, the geographical and topological aspects of his fowling grounds. To illustrate this latter point, geese flighted in the morning by a fowler ensconced on the south-east shore of an estuary will have the light of the rising sun reflected off their flanks as they head inland. Quite different in appearance is the same species seen by a gunner on the north-west shore, to whom the birds will be silhouetted against the morning light as they flight in from the tideline to feed in the fields on his side of the water.

MALLARD: Strong, fairly fast level flight with rapid wing beats; large size; drake normally silent in flight, duck emits the familiar low 'quack'.

WIGEON: Rapid flight with wings often appearing sickle-shaped; medium size; light belly and white shoulders; short bill; cock gives a high pitched whistle while the hen has a low purr.

TEAL: Very rapid flight with small flocks frequently rising and dipping in unison; small size; the male has a 'prip-prip' call while the female 'quacks' at a slightly higher pitch than a mallard.

PINTAIL: Fast flight with very rapid wing beats; medium to large size; male has characteristic 'pin' tail but both sexes are long, slender birds with slightly sickle-shaped wings; male gives a lower pitched 'prip' than the teal and the duck occasionally emits a rather weak, mallard-like 'quack'.

SHOVELER: Rapid flight with rattling sound from wings; medium size; light blue shoulders prominent in flight; large spatulate bill appears longer than the head; rarely quacks in flight.

TUFTED DUCK: A more fluttery flight than the dabbling duck; small to medium size; males' colour contrast sometimes clear but females' less so; rarely quacks in flight.

POCHARD: Strong, fast flight; medium size; male has low whistle and female occasionally gives out a deep-throated 'Kurr'.

GOLDENEYE: Rapid, direct flight with wing rattle sometimes audible; medium size; light underparts; light cheek patch of male usually visible in flight; normally silent.

SHELDUCK: (Protected) Strong, goose-like flight; large size; contrasting markings usually visible; male occasionally whistles, female has short, low 'quack'.

EIDER: (Protected) Strong flight, often with apparent 'nose-down' aspect; large size; frequently flies very close to the ground; coarse voice.

GREYLAG: Large goose with heavy head and bill more obvious in flight than with other geese; pale grey shoulders; white rump; low 'aung-aung' call similar to farmyard goose.

PINKFOOT: Medium-sized goose with dark head; more slender than greylag in flight; darker underparts than greylag; familiar 'wink-wink' call.

WHITEFRONT: (Protected in Scotland) Medium to large size; black barring on lower breast; darker, more slender head than greylag; high-pitched 'hank-hank-hank' call.

CANADA GOOSE: Large heavy goose with black head and white chinstrap; light underparts; 'honk-honk' call gives it the American nickname 'honker'.

BARNACLE: (Protected) Smallish goose with white face and black breast; rarely flies in formation, preferring loose flocks; voice sounds like the 'yipping' of a pack of small dogs.

BRENT: (Protected) Small goose appearing to have a black head and chest and dark underparts in flight; fast wingbeats, frequently flying in tight packs or, more occasionally, in formation; normally silent in flight and more likely to be mistaken for a large duck than for any other goose.

Identification Plates

As an aid to wildfowl identification in field conditions, the identification plates between pages 87 and 88 have been prepared to illustrate a number of the standard keys which can flash a message to the fowler's brain as a bird streaks toward him in the half light. By and large, wildfowl are not vividly coloured birds and if the plates are held at arm's length, the characteristic meld of brown and grey tones will predominate. This is the best that a wildfowler can hope to distinguish when a bird is in the air. Closer examination of the plates will reveal the typical coloration which can be seen once the retriever has brought the shot fowl to hand.

Plates 1–7, illustrating the duck species, are all drawn to the same scale while Plate 8, depicting the geese, is reduced by a further twenty-five per cent. In this chapter, on the other hand, the silhouettes have been drawn with the same body length in every case. This treatment serves to show the differing ratios of wing to body and varying relative sizes of head, body, wings and tail. Unless the fowler has definite reference points against which to assess range, it is those aspect ratios which, together with flight pattern and tone and colour keys, will identify the species. Once the bird has been identified, relative size will enable the wildfowler to judge range.

To a large extent the identification problems facing a wildfowler are dictated by the part of the country in which he follows his sport. Mallard, wigeon and teal are fairly universal but each is fairly easily distinguished from the common protected species of shelduck and eider. It is mainly in south-east England that the fowler need worry about brent geese while the Solway gunner requires to be on his guard against firing a shot at a barnacle goose. In the north-east of Britain the wildfowler can be fairly confident that any largish goose he comes across will be either a greylag or pinkfoot and, as both are shootable and edible, misidentification is not criminal. Even in this case, however, he should have been able to differentiate on voice alone if the light was insufficient to provide visible clues.

When a howling gale is whipping over the foreshore and the first grey streaks of dawn begin to lighten the eastern sky, it takes both skill and resolve to identify the dark shape which flipped past one's right shoulder, bring up the gun and pull the trigger — all in the correct sequence! Every fowler makes an occasional genuine mistake early in his career on the marsh. Provided that he learns from his errors and makes a conscious effort to 'identify first — shoot second', no great harm has been done although, having said that, there is no guarantee that a law court will take a similar view. It is the gunner who neither knows the difference between a mallard and a shelduck nor really cares, the man who regards anything which flies as a target for his shotgun, who is a menace on the saltings. If wildfowling is to remain an honoured and legitimate activity in Britain the statutes of the land must be observed, the sensibilities of bird protectionists considered and, most important of all, the quarry afforded the respect which such fine creatures undoubtedly deserve.

6

A Gun for the Marsh

On the reedy north shore of the Tay estuary there is a little natural harbour named Port Allen. Being serviced by a metalled road, it is one of the few places on the Firth where ready vehicular access is available to the foreshore without the requirement of obtaining permission from private landowners. In consequence, it is an extremely popular spot with visiting fowlers and, as a result, the geese flighting in from the off-shore mudbanks become very wary indeed. As in many other areas where shooting pressure is particularly heavy, the only real chance of good sport occurs when the weather turns especially wild. With a raging gale there is a possibility that at least some of the skeins will pass within range of a waiting wildfowler.

Faced with fowl which habitually fly high, there is a tendency to seek a combination of gun and cartridge which will be effective at maximum range. Very often this imagined solution takes precedence over potentially more fruitful strategies such as developing one's concealment skills so as to get closer to the start of the flightlines. In my own case, I was convinced that those tall Port Allen greylag would be brought within range if only I could acquire a massive four-bore shoulder gun. I never did realise that

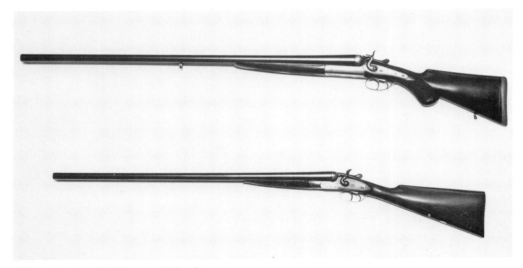

8-bore (top) and 12-bore wildfowling gun.

ambition to own a double-four but, over the years, almost every other size and shape of fowling piece has passed through my hands.

An early acquisition was a double-barrelled ten-bore chambered for 3½-inch magnum cartridges. The power to project 2¼ ounces of lead shot skywards was, I thought, a sure answer to the problem of stratospheric geese and, despite the inordinately high cost of factory-loaded cartridges, I purchased a couple of boxes and set off for the fowling grounds. That gun did score some notable successes but it also taught me that firepower is less important than accuracy when it comes to shooting geese and duck.

One morning, not long after I obtained the ten-bore, I was comfortably settled in the shelter of a hawthorn bush on the sea wall not far from Port Allen. My memory is that it was a cold, crisp morning with little breeze to bring the birds down to a respectable height. The music of the geese carried clearly over the estuary and I looked forward to the flight with a little more confidence than usual. On mornings such as those there is much to see while waiting for the wildfowl to leave their roost and it was my habit to take along a small sketch pad upon which I could jot random thoughts or, perhaps, make a drawing which reflected the mood of the day. I remember quite clearly that I was sketching a blue-tit hanging upside down from a swaying reed stalk when a change of note in the goose music signalled that some birds were in the air.

I slipped two of the long green Remington cartridges into the chambers of my gun and the noise of the breech snapping shut sent the blue-tit flitting ten yards along the sea wall. On the skeins came and, from their direction, it became clear that I would be unlikely to get a shot. Most passed several hundred yards to the east but, just as I was about to again sit down on the sea wall, a small group of ten or twelve greys changed course and headed straight for my position. Gripping the oiled stock of the big gun even tighter I waited until the leading bird was almost overhead and then, judging their range to be between forty and forty-five yards, I swung up the 32-inch barrels and squeezed the front trigger. Pulling on to another goose, I let a second charge of No.1 shot fly skywards and, almost immediately, felt that dull sinking feeling as the entire skein flew on unscathed.

Dejectedly, I watched them flight over the wide stubble field behind the sea wall, gaining height all of the time, until the double crack of a light twelve-bore gun sounded from the edge of the rear of the field. Amazed, I witnessed two greylag fall from the skein. One bird was stone dead but the other swung around towards the estuary and cleared the sea wall before crashing into the dense reed beds not far from my position. Scrapie, my yellow labrador bitch, was sent to retrieve the goose and, upon safely despatching the bird, I clambered down the landward side of the wall to deliver it to the figure who was now walking across the stubble.

It transpired that the man was a gamekeeper on the Errol estate and had been out to shoot hoodies and magpies when the geese appeared overhead. Although the skein must have been fully fifty yards high when it passed over his hedgerow, two geese had succumbed to charges of No.4 shot fired from the keeper's perfectly ordinary game gun. At a lesser range, I had obviously cleanly missed the greylag with my oversized fowling piece.

The tendency to keep changing guns in an attempt to find an answer to high flying wildfowl can be counter-productive. 'Gunitis' is a common disease among the fowling fraternity, and as a chronic affliction it can weigh heavily upon the bank balance. Fortunately there is a cure for those with the resolve to sweat out the fever; a remedy which involves not only making a hard, cool appraisal of all the known information about gun and cartridge performance but also accepting that the theoretical solutions are likely to prove effective in practice.

To be so coldly clinical is to deny the fowler the pleasure of handling a variety of guns but it is perhaps better for the newcomer to the sport to achieve a high level of competence with a single shotgun before experimenting with a wider range. The alternative is to give way to romantic notions of exaggerated firepower rather than objectively assessing the factors which determine the weapon which will produce optimum results in the majority of wildfowling circumstances. If you are lured by the prospect of emulating our forefathers and using a large-bore shotgun then, by all means, go out and slay your quarry with the gun of your fancy. But when your back aches with the weight of the piece and your pocket complains at the cost of the cartridges it consumes, then perhaps you may be persuaded to give a little thought to the principles which govern the effectiveness of a shotgun.

Calibres of Gun

The range of guns available to the fowler is wide and each has its band of devotees. Traditionally, the larger bore weapons were favoured for use below the sea wall and many of those mighty pieces are carefully preserved by proud owners as relics of the past. To all intents and purposes the four-bore and eight-bore are guns for enthusiasts who have the time and money to load their own cartridges. Ralph Grant of Leicester has introduced a modern single-barrelled four-bore and a double eight-bore to the British market but most of the shotguns in those calibres are older examples of the English gunmaking trade. Several distributors import double-barrelled ten-bores but the great majority of shotguns in regular use in Britain today are twelve-bores in one of a variety of configurations.

As a matter of interest, the bore 'number' of a shotgun is derived from the reciprocal of the weight in pounds of a spherical ball of lead which has a diameter equivalent to that of the gun barrel. Thus a four-bore has a barrel of the same diameter as a $\frac{1}{4}$-lb ball of lead and a twelve-bore barrel will allow a ball of lead weighing $\frac{1}{12}$-lb to pass along it. The bore sizes for which cartridges are normally available in Britain are ten, twelve, sixteen, twenty and twenty-eight gauges, together with the ·410 which departs from the general rule and is simply a measurement in inches. It should be noted that the reciprocal weight formula is normally fairly exact for guns of twelve-bore and smaller, but some of the older models of large gauge shotgun vary in their compliance to the rule. A number of eight-bores, for example, have chambers which are of the correct eight-bore size, but have barrels which are of slightly smaller diameter than the formula would predict.

4-, 8-, 10- and 12-bore wildfowling cartridges.

Cartridges

It has been stated on many occasions, usually when reinforcing rules of safety, that it is not the gun which kills but, rather, two or three pellets of lead from a cartridge which the gun merely holds, detonates and directs. The logical consequence of this truism is to defer further consideration of the weapon itself until some thought has been given to the ammunition which may be best suited to our sport. Thereafter we will be in a position to look for a gun which is adequate to fire the cartridge which we have chosen.

In this chapter I will attempt to avoid confounding or boring the reader with mathematical formulae relating to ballistic theory. There are many excellent books available which cover this subject in detail and a couple are mentioned in Appendix A. Suffice it to note at this stage that the killing power of a cartridge at any set range is a function of two factors — pattern density and pellet striking energy. In this connection it is vital to recognise that the maximum effective range of a cartridge is limited by whichever of those two factors *fails first*. Thus, if pattern density falls off before striking energy, the maximum range at which the cartridge can be expected to give a clean kill is dictated by the former parameter. Conversely, if striking energy drops below a calculated minimum at a certain range, no benefit can be drawn from the fact that pattern density may have remained sufficiently tight at greater distances.

Put simply, to ensure a clean kill the quarry must be hit by a sufficient number of pellets and must be struck hard enough by each. Only by applying a safe margin of error to such criteria can we be sure that a vital organ of the bird will be damaged and a kill secured. The table which follows makes use of accepted ballistic data to provide maximum effective ranges for varying cartridge loads when used against geese. All are calculated on the basis of being fired from a full choke barrel but this factor is, in fact, unimportant in relative terms.

Maximum effective range of cartridges for geese

Shot Load (oz.)	Shot Size	Max. Range (yards)	Limiting Factor
1⅛	4	40	Striking energy
1⅛	3	50	Both equally
1¼	3	50	Striking energy
1¼	1	42	Pattern density
1¼	BB	35	Pattern density
1½	3	50	Striking energy
1½	1	47	Pattern density
1½	BB	38	Pattern density
1⅝	1	50	Pattern density
1⅝	BB	40	Pattern density
1⅞	1	53	Pattern density
1⅞	BB	43	Pattern density

Note: American No. 2 shot is equivalent to British No. 1.

The tabulation covers most of the cartridge loads currently available in Britain and suggests that the greatest effective range is obtained by using a magnum load (1⅞ oz) of No.1 shot. It will be noted, however, that the range is only marginally greater than that which could be obtained from an ordinary game load (1⅛ oz) of No.3 shot. Many wildfowlers have become firm believers in the use of BB shot for geese, but the limitations of this large pellet are clear when proper attention is paid to the ranges at which pattern density falls below an acceptable level. Even a three-inch magnum cartridge loaded with 1⅝ oz of BB shot has a maximum effective range of forty-three yards and to risk a shot at greater distances would be to rely upon the chance of a single pellet causing fatal damage in defiance of the law of averages.

Not only is the myth of the BB's efficacy exploded; the whole case for magnum loads is exposed to doubt. Accepting that no sportsmanlike wild-fowler would contemplate relying upon fluke kills, it would appear that a standard game load of No.3 shot is as useful a cartridge for the goose shooter as any. By applying similar principles to shot loads for duck, we again find that a good fifty yards effective range can be obtained by employing 1⅛ oz of No.5 or No.6 shot.

There are, of course, many competent fowlers who have favourite cartridge loads which vary from the ideal prescriptions mentioned above. With experience and a consistently moderate assessment of range, they have developed confidence in a certain type of ammunition and achieve excellent results with it. The point which I am attempting to make is that there is no overwhelming need for a magnum gun and heavy cartridges when wildfowl are sought at sporting ranges.

Let me hasten to add that there is one additional factor which determines the maximum range at which the lives of wildfowl will become endangered. Having suggested that relatively light loads of smallish pellets provide the optimum killing power, I will go further and propose that no wildfowler should even consider pulling the trigger if his quarry is at a range which is beyond the limits of his marksmanship skills. In effect, for most of us, forty yards will be a fair maximum and the cartridges which I have suggested for both duck and geese will provide ample reserves in terms of both striking energy and pattern density at that distance.

Choice of Shotgun

This is indeed good news for the novice who is about to purchase his first gun or the established game shot who seeks to extend his range of activities to include wildfowling. As discussed earlier, the gauge of shotgun which is almost universally used in Britain is the twelve-bore and the cartridge loads recommended above can be fired from a normal game gun in that calibre.

I have one very important reason for describing that factor as 'good news'. Having suffered the common wildfowlers' complaint of 'gunitis' and having tried in vain to find a specialist fowling piece which would stretch out to those high duck and geese, I eventually had to concede that the constant advice of the acknowledged gun experts was indeed wisdom worth noting. Briefly, the advice which I scorned for so long but which I now pass on confidently is the simple statement that a man will shoot best if he uses the same gun for all his sport. Clearly the serious clay pigeon shot, who will want specialist guns for trap, skeet and other disciplines, must be excluded from this rule but, generally speaking, it will be a decided advantage if the same gun can be employed against pheasant, rabbit, duck and geese. Many professional shooting coaches preach a gospel which states that a man who shoots instinctively will become the best performer. This state will be most readily achieved when the gun virtually becomes an extension of the body so that eye, brain, arms and shotgun are all parts of a single synchronised system. It should be possible to reach this condition most easily if our reflexes are not asked to accommodate the weight, balance and dimensions of more than one gun.

MALLARD

♂

♀

♂

♀

WIGEON

♂

♀

♂

♀

Mallard and Wigeon.

SHOVELER

♂

♀

♂

♀

GADWALL

♂

♀

♂

♀

Shoveler and Gadwall.

BUB

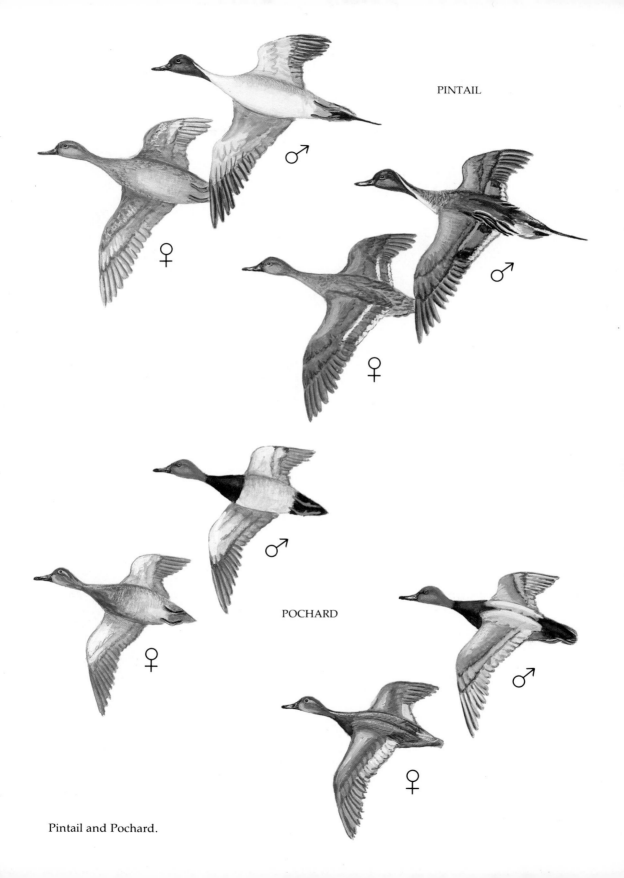

PINTAIL

♂

♀

♂

♀

POCHARD

♂

♀

♂

♀

Pintail and Pochard.

GOLDENEYE

♂

♀

♂

♀

♂

TUFTED DUCK

♀

♂

♀

Goldeneye and Tufted Duck.

BUB

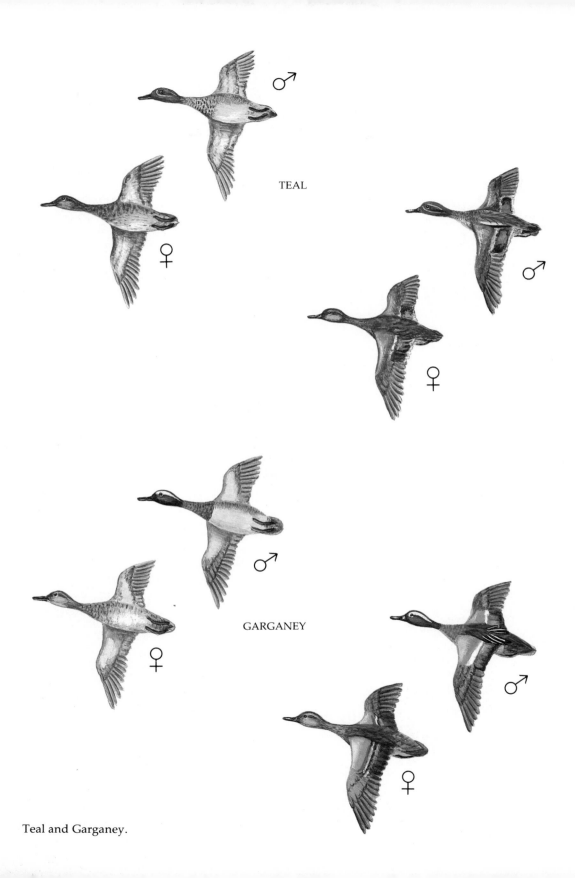

TEAL

♂

♀

♂

♀

GARGANEY

♂

♀

♂

♀

Teal and Garganey.

SHELDUCK

♂

♀

♂

♀

♂

EIDER

♀

♂

♀

Shelduck and Eider.

SCAUP ♂ ♀

LONG-TAILED DUCK ♀ ♂

♂ (In Summer)

COMMON SCOTER ♂ ♀

VELVET SCOTER ♂ ♀

Scaup, Long-tailed Duck,
Common Scoter and Velvet Scoter.

BwB

BEAN

GREYLAG

PINKFOOTED

EUROPEAN WHITEFRONT

GREENLAND WHITEFRONT

LIGHT BELLIED BRENT

CANADA

DARK BELLIED BRENT

BARNACLE

Various Geese.

BWB

I have greatly enjoyed shooting with borrowed four-bore and eight-bore fowling pieces and would not wish to detract from the romance which is associated with large guns. In terms of looking for a regular armament with which to begin a fowling career, however, there is much to be said for selecting a twelve-bore and using it for roughshooting, game shooting and informal claybusting as well as for wildfowling. By shooting frequently at a variety of quarry, one will soon develop a high standard of skill.

Even the decision to employ a standard twelve-bore for all his shooting does not relieve the tyro of other choices. There still remains the question of barrel configuration about which to worry and matters such as choke borings still have to be resolved.

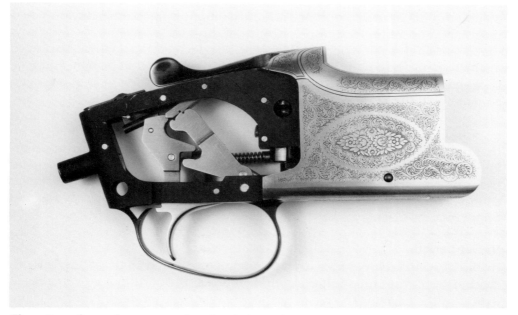

The action of a modern over-and-under shotgun. (*Photograph: courtesy Frank Dyke & Co Ltd*)

Barrel Configuration

For many years the conventional side-by-side shotgun was favoured for virtually every kind of shooting and it reached a state of both technical and aesthetic perfection which no other type has yet overtaken. The traditional English design has been successfully copied by gunmakers in Spain, Italy, America and Japan with the result that good serviceable specimens may be found throughout a very wide price range. Available as boxlocks or sidelocks and as ejectors or non-ejectors, side-by-side guns are quick to reload, can be very well balanced and are simple to break down for cleaning.

The over-and-under was popularised by clay pigeon shooters but is now regarded as an acceptable alternative for all branches of the sport. Most models have a single selective trigger which is a decided bonus when shooting with gloved hands. Other advantages claimed by supporters of the over-and-under are the single sighting plane and the fact that the lower plane of the bottom barrel, which is normally fired first, helps to prevent gun-flip and hence assists second barrel accuracy. The wider gape to which an over-and-under requires to be opened does, however, make reloading a slightly slower and more fiddly process than with a side-by-side. For guns of similar quality, an over-and-under will tend to be a little more expensive than a side-by-side.

Semi-automatic and pump action repeaters were once popular with wildfowlers and roughshooters on account of their relatively low cost and the imagined advantage of increased firepower. Few are as well balanced as a good double barrelled gun and they are more prone to malfunction when used in the muddy conditions encountered by the estuarine fowler. Now that the *Wildlife and Countryside Act 1981* has decreed that, when employed against game birds or wildfowl, the magazine of a repeater must be plugged so as to accept no more than two cartridges, their appeal has been considerably reduced. An additional problem to the repeating shotgun user was posed by the *Firearms (Amendment) Act 1988* which stipulated that such a gun could only be held on a Shotgun Certificate if it had been manufactured with a magazine capacity of not more than two cartridges or, alternatively, had been permanently converted to meet this condition and the conversion had been certified by a Proof House. Any automatic or pump action shotgun with a greater magazine capacity must now be held on a Firearms Certificate.

Barrel Length

In the age of black powder it was generally accepted that, within reason, the performance of a shotgun would improve proportionally to increased length of the barrels. To an extent there was some foundation for this claim as black powder burned slowly and progressively with the result that the longer the wad and shot charge took to travel up the barrel, the more efficient would be the utilisation of the energy released by the burning gunpowder. Within the limits of modern shotgun design, there is no significant ballistic advantage to be gained from long barrels when using cartridges loaded with fast burning nitro powders. To all intents and purposes, therefore, the choice of barrel length can be solely concerned with gun balance and shooting style.

The great majority of twelve-bore shotguns on the market today have barrels of between twenty-five inches and thirty-two inches in length. Guns with twenty-five-inch or twenty-six-inch barrels are supposed to be faster handling and particularly suited to fast, short range birds, whereas thirty-inch or thirty-two-inch barrelled weapons are usually sold with the claim that they will produce an exaggerated swing when used against high pheasants or geese. There is a certain logic in those statements but, as most wildfowlers will use the same gun to shoot at a teal flipping past at twenty yards and greylag flighting over at forty yards, it could be a mistake to opt for either extreme.

Another consideration is chamber length and this is directly related to the type of cartridges which it is intended to use. Almost all modern imported twelve-bores will have 2¾-inch or three-inch chambers but, if a secondhand English gun is being considered, it may have shorter chambers and the selection of cartridges will be correspondingly restricted.

Choke

The question of choke is one which is not fully understood by many gun users and the current vogue amongst wildfowlers for very tight choke borings reflects this lack of appreciation. By the term choke we mean the amount of constriction towards the muzzle end of a shotgun barrel which the gunmaker has incorporated to reduce the spread of the pellets. The relative effect of various degrees of choke is shown in the following table.

The effect of choke on pattern speed

Choke Boring	Nominal Constriction (thou ")	Diameter of Spread at 40 yards
True cylinder	—	58 inches
Improved cylinder	5	51 inches
¼-choke	10	48 inches
½-choke	20	45 inches
¾-choke	30	42 inches
Full choke	40	40 inches

It is widely assumed that there is an advantage to be gained from a full choke barrel which can be directly translated into increased killing power. In fact, if we are willing to accept a marksmanship limit of around forty yards — and that is quite a long distance — then tight choke borings are likely to *reduce* the chance of obtaining a clean kill. At the range of forty yards a barrel which is bored improved cylinder, i.e. only five points of choke, will throw fifty per cent of the pellets within a thirty-inch diameter circle. With the 1⅛-oz loads of No. 3 or No. 5 shot recommended earlier, this provides an adequate pattern for geese and duck respectively. The effect of a tighter choke boring would simply be to reduce the spread of the shot and, accordingly, would demand a higher degree of accuracy to secure a kill.

This conclusion presents yet another piece of good news as the standard twelve-bore game gun is normally bored either improved cylinder/half choke or ¼-choke/¾-choke. Once again we find support for the view that a gun designed for general game shooting is a perfectly adequate weapon for service below the sea wall.

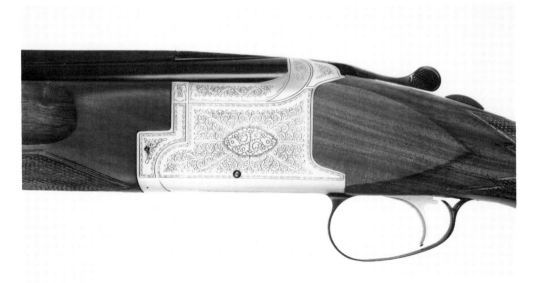

A good wood-to-metal fit will help to prevent deterioration. *(Photograph: courtesy Frank Dyke & Co Ltd)*

Since the first edition of this book was published, a number of excellent multichoke shotguns have become available and some of these are available with three-inch chambers and are proofed for magnum cartridges. Guns of this type can be very versatile and, bearing in mind that wildfowling is a very individualistic sport about which no one person holds a monopoly of wisdom, the man who does have faith in tighter chokes and heavier shot loads for wildfowling can now use the same gun on the shore as he employs with game borings and light cartridges for pheasant or woodpigeon shooting.

Incidentally, it is often assumed that only low quality shotguns should be subjected to the rigours of the shore and that any sportsman should think twice before exposing a fine weapon to the salt and mud of a tidal estuary. In actual fact, the opposite thesis is more sustainable. Poorly finished guns tend to suffer most readily from corrosion and the cheaper materials used in such guns will be less able to withstand hard usage. Certainly good English shotguns together with those by reputable foreign manufacturers such as AYA, Beretta, Browning and Laurona have proven records of long service in the hands of coastal wildfowlers.

Proof

No discussion about guns would be complete without mention of the question of proof. By law every shotgun sold in Britain, whether new or secondhand, must be in proof and must bear the proof marks of either the London or Birmingham Proof House or one of the recognised foreign proof authorities. The existence of proof marks on an old or well used gun does not in itself guarantee that the weapon is still in proof or is safe to use.

Deterioration or enlargement of the bores, for instance, could render a gun out of proof. Many old shotguns were only proved for use with black powder and should not be used with modern smokeless cartridges. The owner of such a piece really has no alternative than to send the gun, through his gunsmith, to the Proof House to be reproved for use with nitro powder cartridges. If he does not wish to risk the gun being blown apart in the hands of the Proofmaster, he must recognise that it can only be used with black powder cartridges or, perhaps more realistically, deactivated and relegated to hang as a wall ornament. When buying a secondhand shotgun it is essential to obtain the opinion of a reputable gunsmith and so avoid the fate of the gentleman described in the following rhyme.

LACK OF PROOF

Did you hear the tragedy of Jeremiah Dunn
Who to the Olde Shoppe went to find a gun?
'A fine one we have here, Sir
A genuine antique
With hammers, long brown barrels
And a pedigree unique.'

'It killed ten thousand pheasants for Lord Barchester they say,
And many more besides, for his son the young Merleigh.
They make them not like this, Sir,
In modern times, I'm sure.
A better piece you'll never find
From here to Walton Moor.'

Our hero gladly paid the price. He would have offered more.
Then strapped the gun across his back and strode towards the shore.
'Those geese will soon be mine now,'
He thought while on his way.
'Those magnums in my pocket.
Shall surely earn their pay.'

The first shot that our Jerry fired near knocked him off his feet.
The second threw him backwards to land upon his seat.
But not dismayed he scrambled up,
Pushed more shells in the breech.
'Those longer ones must surely
Bring the ducks within my reach.'

The ending of this story to tell might seem quite harsh.
But Jeremiah's ashes are strewn across the marsh.
The gun blew up, we knew it would.
The moral's clear in truth.
Never, never buy a gun
Which may not be in Proof.

Care of Shotguns

Having obtained the weapon of his choice, the wildfowler must take a few elementary precautions to ensure that his gun lasts him for many years. Of all forms of shooting wildfowling is, by its very nature, potentially hardest on a gun. Mud and salt water are the twin enemies of any mechanical device and both abound in the fowler's environment. Firstly, it certainly pays dividends to purchase both a hard case and a soft gunslip. The former will give adequate protection against knocks and bumps while the gun is being transported in the boot of a car while the gunslip will be more practical for carrying over one's shoulder in the field. It is important that the gunslip be fleece-lined to avoid the blueing being rubbed off the muzzle-ends of the barrels as can happen with a plain canvas cover. It is equally vital that a full-length zip is fitted in order that the slip may be fully opened to permit the lining to dry after use. If the hard case has space for a cleaning rod, rag and a couple of boxes of cartridges, so much the better.

Proper care of the gun is a three phase affair. In the first place, before putting it away in the car after shooting, a few squirts of an 'instant maintenance' spray lubricant such as WD-40 should be directed down the barrels and over external metalwork. A quick rub down with a rag will then remove any surplus moisture. On reaching home, clean the gun thoroughly. I find that another squirt of WD-40 down each barrel, followed by pushing through a rolled-up ball of soft toilet tissue, is usually more than enough to remove all deposits from the chambers and bores although, more from tradition than anything else, I give a good scrub with a phosphor-bronze brush and old-fashioned gun oil once or twice each season. The third stage of maintenance is an annual strip down, inspection and clean by a competent gunsmith. If you develop the right sort of relationship with your local man, the gun need be out of your hands for less than a week for this vital operation. At the time of writing my own Beretta is ten years old, has fired in excess of 20,000 cartridges and, although the woodwork is now badly scored, there is no rust and the gun has never misfired. If simple maintenance can provide such a degree of reliability, then surely the steps outlined above must be well worthwhile.

Finally, we must give some consideration to shotgun security. Unfortunately, there are no national standards and local police forces may differ in the degree of security which they demand. Even before security conditions were attached to the granting of a Shotgun Certificate, however, responsible wildfowlers protected their guns from damage or theft and there is much to be said for a purpose-built steel security cabinet which can be bolted to a solid wall and kept locked. There is not only the threat of burglary but also the possibility that children might interfere with a shotgun — a ploy which can have tragic consequences. Ammunition should similarly be kept in a safe place.

In many ways it seems a pity to have so many regulations imposed upon the legitimate shotgun owner. We certainly live in a very different world from that experienced by the old-time fowlers from whom we inherited our sport. Once out on the estuary, however, we can forget many of the constraints of the modern world and, whether our gun is a contemporary over-and-under or an ancient large bore fowling piece, we can forge a link with the spirits of the sportsmen of bygone times and enjoy the essential solitude of the marsh.

7
Clothing and Equipment

In the early days of my wildfowling career it seemed that the prevailing ethos demanded that the pursuit of fowl below the sea wall be carried out in conditions of self imposed suffering. According to the dogma of the day, no self respecting fowler would give a thought to his own comfort and, if the geese failed to oblige by flighting within range, at least there was the satisfaction of frozen fingers or damp hindquarters to make the expedition worthwhile. If the pundits who wrote in the country sports magazines were to be believed, deprivation, hardship and a good measure of discomfort were all considered to be intrinsic parts of the sport.

There was one January morning which really taught me that the sensible fowler should do everything within his power to reduce discomfort on the saltings. The weather had been hard for over a week and inland lochs were solid with ice. In those circumstances, there is always the chance of some good sport if one can arrange a visit to the estuary before the fowl begin to suffer from the reduced feeding which sometimes results from extremely low temperatures.

On the morning in question Andrew and I had driven up to the Tay hoping against hope that many of the geese which normally frequented the reservoirs and lochs in the area would have been forced down to salt water by the cold spell. On that score we were not to be disappointed. Having parked the car at the western approach to Kingoodie Bay, we made our way through the dense reeds and, with the frozen vegetation crunching noisily beneath our wadered feet, set out over the saltgrass to a favourite creek. In the still morning air the music of a thousand grey geese travelled over a mile of foreshore to gladden our hearts.

We were faced with a very long and uncomfortable wait. For some unaccountable reason the geese were in no hurry to flight that morning and the tide was slowly filling the gully in which we had sought to hide. With the tide at full ebb it was possible to stand upright in that creek but, as the water flowed slowly but surely, we were forced to kneel and then to crouch in order to avoid our heads bobbing up above the bank and scaring every goose on the shore. For almost two hours we huddled against the gully wall, our only consolation being that the very mud had frozen and some-what less of the sticky, slimy stuff transferred itself on to our persons, our guns and our dogs than might otherwise have been the case. It was one of the coldest mornings that I can recall in over a quarter of a century of wildfowling and it was the first occasion upon which I experienced that strange eeriness of the crackling of pack ice in a gully as the tide rises under it.

Eventually the birds did grow restless and a few small parties traversed the foreshore to cross the sea wall half a mile to the east of our position. Then, with the winter's sun well above the horizon, four or five hundred greys lifted from directly in front of the creek and headed towards us. To cut a short story even shorter, our limbs and fingers were so cold that Andrew succeeded in getting only one shot off — and that was well wide of the mark — while I could not even get to my feet and raise the gun to my shoulder before the skeins were far out of range.

Such follies now lie in the past and, in recent years, I have made no excuses for researching ways and means of keeping warm and dry on the marsh. It is without apology to any readers who may think that it is 'macho' to face the rigours of a British winter without adequate clothing that this chapter deals fairly comprehensively with the apparel and equipment which can make the wildfowler's vigil a little more comfortable. The tale which I related above may be an extreme case, but there can be little argument with the view that the unchilled fowler's standard of marksmanship will be rather higher than that of the man who suffers from leaden feet and numbed fingers. Despite the opinions which prevailed in my youth, I no longer accept that it is any way a betrayal of the traditions of our sport to seek to avoid the privations which, of necessity, were part of the lives of the professional fowlers of a hundred years ago. All the aid which modern technology can provide does not detract from the magic of rising from bed in the early hours of a winter morning and pursuing duck and geese below the sea wall in the wild, wild world of a dawning estuary.

Clothing

Until recently, it was difficult for a wildfowler to select one outfit which would suit all of the weather conditions he might meet on the marsh. Many of us attempted to make do with one outer coat and, indeed, many of the country clothing manufacturers produced garments which appeared to have been designed by statistical calculation. I suspect that some clothing technologist had fed reams of data into his computer and discovered that the average shooting day had a mean temperature of 7°C, a wind speed of 14.85 knots and 0.45 inches of rain. A shooting coat was then carefully designed and mass-produced to suit those conditions. Unfortunately, that average shooting day occurs just as infrequently as the mallard which lays the average clutch of 9¾ eggs!

In the first edition of *Modern Wildfowling* I attempted to overcome this difficulty by pointing out that during the course of a wildfowling season we

Dressed for the mud. *(Photograph: courtesy J. Barbour & Sons Ltd)*

may be faced with weather which is mild and wet or, alternatively, conditions which are cold and dry. It is exceedingly rare for the British climate to mix very wet weather with extremely low temperatures and, hence, the fowler is normally faced with only one weather problem at a time. It seemed logical, therefore, to modify one's wildfowling attire according to whether the object is to keep dry in the face of heavy rainfall or to retain body heat in conditions of hard frost.

There may still be some merit in remembering that we must dress to combat extremes of weather but, in general terms, recent advances in the country clothing field have made our task a little easier. Modern synthetic fibres can result in totally waterproof outer clothing, while high quality thermal underwear is able to guard us against sub-zero temperatures. Let us not forget that the cream of coastal wildfowling can occur when a force-9 gale drives torrential rain across the foreshore. Not only does a fierce storm tend to bring the geese and duck within range of the shore gunner and, in consequence, provide sporting shooting; there is the added advantage that the estuary is likely to be less crowded with faint-hearted fowlers under such conditions. In reality, they do not know what they are missing. Not only are the fowl much more obliging on such mornings but there is a primitive satisfaction to be gained from being in a position of tenuous security at the height of a storm. My memory travels back to childhood when there was much more pleasure to be obtained by sheltering from a downpour in the doorway of a garden shed than by seeking the complete sanctuary of the house. In youth also, the cosiness of being in a relatively dry tent while rain pelted the canvas was part of the joy of camping. Similarly, the wildfowler snugly ensconced in a gully on the marsh, well wrapped in waterproof clothing, experiences the same all-pervading sense of quiet contentment as the elements rage around him. The key to such enjoyment is, of course, that one's clothing must be suited to the task in hand.

Headwear

In selecting an outfit for the well-dressed wildfowler it seems logical to start at the top and consider first the question of headwear. It is not without good reason that almost every shooting sportsman has some form of hat perched on his cranium. It goes without saying that a hat is useful for keeping the head dry in rainy conditions, but not everyone appreciates that it also has a vital role to play in heat conservation. On a cold day, especially if there is a strong wind, a great deal of energy can be dissipated through the veins which run close to the skin on top of the skull. Presumably those of us whose natural thatch is wearing a bit thin will be even more adversely affected if an insulating layer of tweed or wool is not worn.

Two other purposes served by a suitably designed hat are to shade the eyes from the sun and throw a shadow over the fowler's face. This latter aspect is particularly important on the marsh at sunrise or sunset because the white orb of a human physiog can very easily flash an early warning to any approaching duck or geese.

Many wildfowlers opt for a forage cap or balaclava helmet. A camouflaged cap with a decent peak can be useful but few are really waterproof. A balaclava is also likely to lack waterproofing and, although very warm, suffers from the additional disadvantage of covering the fowler's ears and perhaps slightly impairing the essential sense of hearing. The standard hood which is often fitted to waterproof jackets tends not to be particularly effective for use while actually shooting and that old sportsman's favourite, the fore-and-aft deerstalker, has a rear peak which is almost guaranteed to catch on the fowler's coat collar and push the hat over his eyes just as the trigger is about to be pulled on an overhead bird. One type of headwear which has made a welcome return to the market and which can meet most of a wildfowler's requirements is the waxed cotton sou'wester, which is manufactured by Barbour.

I am sure that there would be a high level of demand for a purpose-designed wildfowler's hat and perhaps some enterprising manufacturer might like to take the hint. Failing that, the keen longshore gunner might be able to persuade the lady in his life to set to work with a needle and thread. The ideal hat would be fashioned out of a waterproof material and be dyed a matt mixture of green, brown and straw. To shade the wild-fowler's face and help keep rain out of his eyes it would be fitted with a large peak and to prevent water from running down his neck it should be furnished with a substantial flap to overlap his coat collar. To avoid the hat being blown off by a sudden gust of wind or falling off when a high shot is taken, a chinstrap should be provided but, of course, the fowler's ears must remain uncovered.

What we would seem to have designed is a camouflaged version of the famous legionnaires' *képi* and one is almost tempted to add a hatband into which a few stalks of grass or reeds might be inserted to complete the picture. There is certainly no reason why a face veil should not be incorporated in such a manner that it could be tucked away inside the cap when not required.

Jackets and Trousers
Working down from the neck, the next outer garment to which we must turn our attention is the topcoat or jacket and here we meet a bewildering choice of garments and an exceedingly wide range of prices.

At the least expensive end of the market are a number of lightweight coats manufactured from nylon or similar polymers. The best may be truly waterproof but many, officially classed as 'showerproof', will allow damp- ness through the fabric in heavy rain. Using similar fabrics but paying greater attention to detail are some nice jackets by suppliers, such as Perfectos and Peter Storm, in which sophisticated techniques are used to incorporate both waterproof outer layers and heat-retaining linings. One drawback attributed to many of the coats which use nylon material is that they tend to be noisy if crinkled or brushed against bushes. This may not be a serious disadvantage to the wildfowler who generally takes up his position and then remains still but it will not be welcomed by the sports- man who wishes to wear the same garment for roughshooting or deerstalking.

Many wildfowlers continue to place their faith in the traditional thorn- proof waxed cotton jacket which has been a firm favourite with the shooting community for several decades. The material is not in itself a hundred per cent waterproof but, provided that it is redressed regularly with a proprietary proofing compound, a very high degree of weather protection can be obtained. Brand names such as Barbour, Belstaff, Thorndale and Keeperwear are well known, and many of their products have recently become popular as town-wear in addition to their more functional use in the shooting field. Oiled or waxed cotton is virtually silent but it does tend to be a little heavier than many of the synthetic fabrics. Another slight problem experienced by some fowlers is that, after a hard walk out on to the marsh, they may be sweating inside their waxed cotton coat. The condensation cannot readily escape and, in due course, their damp bodies begin to chill as they patiently await the fowl.

This particular difficulty is overcome by some of the new high- technology fabrics such as Goretex. Coats manufactured from this material can be lightweight, very warm, completely waterproof and the lining allows body moisture to pass out without allowing rain water to pass in. My particular favourite is a shooting coat from the Musto Country range, which has all the features I require and provides the bonus of having a totally matt finish. Garments such as this do tend to be rather expensive but they are suitable for all weather conditions and, if properly cared for, should last for many seasons.

Whatever type is chosen, there are certain factors to consider before deciding to purchase the product of any particular manufacturer. Some jackets are far too short to provide real protection and a useful guide in this respect is to check that the hem of the coat overlaps your wader tops by at least three or four inches. By the same token, ensure that the sleeves cover your wrists and that the storm cuffs are effective. For obvious reasons a double-ended zip is essential and a generous storm flap should cover it. Personally I prefer dull gunmetal press studs to the more modern Velcro fastening on storm flaps and pockets. Make sure that there are adequate pockets both inside and outside and, if you prefer to carry your cartridges loose in a pocket, ensure that the flaps do not impede access for rapid reloading. Finally, it is wise to avoid any topcoat which has been constructed so as to have seams across the shoulders or down the outside of the arms.

There is one black mark which, as far as I can ascertain, has to be awarded against almost all of the manufacturers of shooting waterproofs. It appears that, with only one exception, olive green and brown are still the colours which the makers insist upon presenting to us. Specialised camouflage patterns apart, these dark colours are singularly unsuitable for most shooting purposes and it really is a great pity that no one produces coats or jackets in a light straw colour. Throughout most of the shooting season — whether on the marsh or inland — the predominant hue is of faded vegetation against which any dark object stands out like the proverbial sore thumb. The Barbour Longshoreman fowling smock, introduced in 1990, is the only purpose-designed garment which is of a light enough colour to match those shades.

Overtrousers are available in the same range of materials as jackets and the basic concerns are similar. It is worth searching for a pair which are sufficiently pliable to be tucked inside thigh waders and have enough width in the legs to fit over wellingtons. A design which has side slits to allow access to the pockets of the trousers worn under them is also useful. There are also a number of one-piece suits on the market and, while there may be attractions in terms of weather protection, such a garment does not permit the jacket and trousers to be used independently.

Having examined every shooting jacket and pair of waterproof over-trousers in the shop and finally having made a selection, there are a number of simple rules to be followed in order to maximise the working life of the garments. After each outing any mud should be sponged off and they should be hung to dry in a warm, well ventilated room. Nothing will cause an expensive coat to lose its smart appearance and weatherproof qualities more quickly than being left bundled in the boot of a car after a wet day on the foreshore. Any tears should be repaired immediately using one of the proprietary repair kits and, after one or two seasons hard use, waxproof garments should be reproofed with the manufacturer's water-proofing compound, carefully following the instructions on the tin or aerosol. This operation can be facilitated if the fabric is first warmed by using a hair dryer or giving it a few minutes in a tumble dryer.

Footwear

Many wildfowlers wear thigh boots or fishing waders almost as a matter of course and there are undoubtedly occasions when they are necessary. It follows, therefore, that if financial considerations restrict the fowler to one set of footwear, the clear choice should be a comfortable pair of thick-walled thigh waders with stout cleated soles. It is important not to choose the flimsy design of waders which require to be held up with straps attached to the fowler's belt as they can be difficult to remove quickly if one's feet become trapped in soft mud.

Normally, if I know in advance that I will not be required to wade through deep water, my personal preference is for ordinary wellington boots. Provided that they are worn in conjunction with completely water-

In some situations, thigh waders are helpful.

proof overtrousers, they permit much greater freedom of movement than thigh waders and this can be important to the wildfowler who wishes to crouch, sit or kneel in a confined hidey-hole and jump up to shoot when birds approach.

Gloves

Our individual ability to withstand the effect of very low temperatures on the extremities of the body varies from person to person and it would be cavalier to suggest that every fowler confronted by sub-zero readings on the thermometer should shun the comfort which can be provided by a pair of gloves. While the ancient remedy of dipping one's hands in icy water at the start of an outing actually does succeed in inuring them to the cold, considerable resolve is required to try it out. If gloves or mitts are worn they should be as light and pliable as possible, the type which are made out of very fine leather being particularly suitable. Some, such as the Regal shooting gloves, have a fold-back trigger finger and are excellent in every respect. The user of a gun with a single trigger is less likely to be inconvenienced by wearing gloves than is the man who has to cope with two triggers. One compromise is to have a pair of wristlets which can be wrapped around your wrists and fastened with Velcro. By preventing chilling where the arteries run close to the surface of the skin, wrist-muffs do help to keep the hands warm without in any way interfering with the manipulative facilities of the fingers.

Fingerless mitts and leather shooting gloves.

Underwear

One of the reasons why the modern wildfowler requires only one topcoat to meet all weather conditions is that synthetic fibres such as Goretex allow a fully waterproof coat to be both lightweight and warm. The other reason is the ready availability of top quality thermal underwear. Previously there was a temptation to combat particularly cold weather by merely donning additional sweaters, quilted waistcoats and suchlike. As bulky clothing cannot be other than a hindrance when shooting, it is infinitely preferable to obtain the advantages of extra insulation from lightweight under-garments which have been specifically designed to provide maximum retention of body heat. The best known supplier of thermal underwear is probably Damart and their catalogue contains almost every variety of vests, pants, socks and mitts that the wildfowler is ever likely to require.

It is also worth noting that a woollen or cotton shirt will provide greater heat insulation that one made of nylon and, similarly, a pullover will be warmer if it is knitted from natural, rather than synthetic, fibre. Finally, a soft towelling cravat worn around the neck serves the dual purpose of absorbing rainwater and reducing heat loss.

Equipment

Apart from the clothes which we wear, there are other aids to comfort which warrant consideration. I once achieved a degree of notoriety amongst Tay Estuary wildfowlers by taking a camouflaged deck-chair on to the saltings. It seemed a good idea on paper but, I am afraid, it failed dismally in practice. It was an attempt to provide simultaneous solutions to three difficulties with which many fowlers will be familiar. I had imagined that using a fully extended deck-chair would allow a lower profile to be maintained than is possible with a conventional stool, still keeping a few inches between mud and trousers, while providing a reposed position in which the eyes would be directed at an upward angle to avoid the frequently experienced tragedy of being caught unawares by fowl which inevitably approach while the wildfowler is gazing down at the ground. Unfortunately I was forced to conclude that whereas no duck or geese passed unnoticed, it was not possible to spring out of a deck-chair at the critical moment nor was it easy to shoot while reclining in it.

Seats

Some form of seat can, however, be extremely useful on the foreshore. If reasonably high cover exists or if an artificial hide is being used, the problem may be solved by a portable stool of the type used by coarse anglers and pigeon shooters. The Fife firm of Shooting Developments produces an excellent example which is fully camouflaged in matt paint, is light but sturdy and is very comfortable. If any other model is selected, it may be necessary to paint any bright metal parts with matt green or brown paint to avoid signalling your presence to the fowl.

Even when creek crawling or attempting to become invisible on the open marsh it is an advantage to have some means of raising one's backside an inch or two above the mud. The most convenient solution is a simple seat constructed out of two plywood squares nailed to a light frame of one inch softwood. This can readily be carried in the fowler's bag and avoids the problem of rising damp in the hindquarters.

Bags

Whatever type of bag is employed, it must be sufficiently large to carry all of the fowler's equipment and still have space for a duck or two. An ordinary game bag is unlikely to be sufficiently capacious for anything other than a brief sortie to the estuary and many wildfowlers have discovered that the old style of postman's satchel can provide a useful alternative. They are, however, in increasingly short supply.

Although not universally favoured by wildfowlers, there is a great deal to commend the use of a frame rucksack as both hands are left free and the even distribution of weight across the back means that balance is more easily retained when squelching through soft mud or crossing gutters. Decoys and poles can be hung from the 'D'-rings of a rucksack and it can also be used as a stool in appropriate circumstances.

Binoculars

A good pair of field glasses can be absolutely invaluable for surveying the marsh in daylight while planning a fowling expedition. Unfortunately, many fowlers then leave them in the car when the time comes to set off across the sea wall. It is axiomatic to the very nature of coastal wildfowling that many hours will be spent waiting for the infrequent chance of a shot and such time may be very fruitfully employed if a pair of binoculars is used to examine the wildlife of the estuary. Throughout the day a multitude of waders and other shorebirds will entertain the well-concealed fowler. When choosing a pair of binoculars, do not be tempted to purchase a model which is excessively powerful. For all normal purposes a rating of 7 x 35 or 8 x 40 will be perfectly adequate and a high quality pair which is armoured with waterproof rubber will last a lifetime.

Hearing Protection

Any person who uses a shotgun is liable to suffer from a degree of hearing impairment if he does not take some precautions to protect this vital sense. It is very easy for a young man to imagine that his hearing is suffering no damage but it is amazing how many older sportsmen discover that they are progressively going deaf and regret, too late, that they ignored the advice which was given to them in their youth. Clay pigeon shooters often wear full ear-muffs but bulky apparatus of this type would be inconvenient on the marsh. There are, however, a variety of acoustic ear plugs available to reduce the penetration of the high-frequency sounds which can be so damaging.

The other items of equipment which must be mentioned are concerned mainly with safety and marshcraft and their uses will be considered in the appropriate chapters. Suffice it to note at this point that a reliable compass, a stout staff and a collapsible cleaning rod all have a place on the inventory of the well-equipped wildfowler, as do hides or camouflage netting and a variety of decoys and calls. Knowing how to use those articles is, however, more important than simply possessing them. More of that later.

8
Safety on the Shore

Every shooting sport has its inherent dangers and, traditionally, the first lessons taught to any novice contain a good proportion of instruction in the rules and principles of safety. At close range a shotgun is a particularly lethal weapon, although that is not to say that the effect of a single pellet at over 100 yards should be ignored. Wildfowling, by its very nature, exposes the participant to dangers other than shotgun wounds. Death by drowning or exposure is every bit as final as receiving the force of a charge of shot. The wildfowler, therefore, has two sets of safety rules with which to become thoroughly familiar before taking up his gun and setting foot on the marsh.

During the time that I was secretary of a Fife wildfowling club I arranged for a representative of the local constabulary to attend a club meeting and deliver a lecture on the topic of gun safety. Apart from rendering a very full and enlightening treatment of the subject, the police inspector circulated some photographs of the wounds suffered by shotgun accident victims and it is no exaggeration to say that several strong men became weak-kneed at the sight of the pictures which confronted them. The record of British sportsmen in respect of gun safety is not particularly bad but it must be stressed over and over again that every shooting accident is one too many. Even in safety-conscious Britain it is a simple fact that almost all of the gun accidents which do occur could have been avoided if the elementary rules of safety had been observed. Fortunately, we have not yet reached the situation prevailing in parts of the United States and some European countries where the standard attire of the hunter is a fluorescent orange waistcoat designed to ensure that other sportsmen might readily distinguish its wearer from any of the quarry species.

Safety First

Make no mistake; shotguns are designed to kill and every gunmaking refinement and improvement in cartridge performance is intended to increase that killing efficiency. It is of paramount importance that each person who handles a gun appreciates that he is holding a lethal implement. Gun safety is not only a case of being able to recite the rules; it is an attitude of mind coupled with the constant practice of applied

The wrong way to cross a fence. Is the gun unloaded?

knowledge. Do not merely memorise the following commandments; think about them before you take your gun from the cupboard and consider them constantly while engaged in the shooting field.

Rules of Safety

1 Never point a gun at any person in any circumstances.

2 Treat every gun with the respect due to a loaded gun.

3 Whenever possible, carry your gun in its case or sleeve. When in the field carry it unloaded, with the breech open, until you are in a position to expect a shot.

4 Always unload your gun before crossing any fence, wall, ditch or other obstruction.

5 Check that your gun is unloaded before handing it to anyone, before putting it into a vehicle and before entering a house or other building.

6 Never prop a gun against a wall, vehicle, tree or fence.

7 Always walk with the muzzles pointing at the ground and grip the gun so that you can control the direction of the barrels should you stumble or fall.

8 Never shoot where you cannot see. Long grass, reed beds, bushes and woodland can conceal not only other sportsmen but also foresters, picnickers and courting couples.

9 Before loading your gun, ensure that the barrels are free from obstruction. Mud or snow can block barrels when wildfowling and may cause a fatal burst.

10 Always know where other Guns are concealed and never swing through their positions.

11 Never use a cartridge which may generate a pressure higher than that for which your gun is proof-marked.

12 Keep all guns and ammunition safely locked away from children or inexperienced persons. Never leave a gun in sight in a car.

Every year the toll of casualties from shotgun accidents emphasises the need for complete vigilance when handling firearms of any description. A constantly recurring feature is the number of mishaps or near-mishaps which involve guns which were 'thought to be unloaded'. In all honesty, this is a state of affairs which simply should not exist if the correct drill is followed at all times.

The responsibility for gun safety must override all other considerations in the shooting field, even to the exclusion of normal etiquettes and niceties. On a formal covert shoot any transgression may result in the guilty party being sent home with the utmost despatch and the knowledge that never again will he be invited to the estate in question. Many young Shots have had the principles of safe practice indelibly engraved on their minds and memories by the shame accruing from such a punishment. In wildfowling it may be that such sanctions are not always available but this factor does not relieve the fowler of the duty to draw any dangerous behaviour to the attention of the miscreant. Hopefully this should not be a problem on foreshore which is leased by wildfowling clubs as those clubs will have their own disciplinary codes to deal with unsafe conduct.

For the sake of the peace of mind of your shooting companions it is important not only to be safe but to be seen to be safe. Make every safety check a deliberate, even exaggerated, action so that no one is in any doubt about your conduct. Such behaviour can catch on and your friends and acquaintances may consequently become less of a danger to your own life and limb. By establishing a routine drill of gun safety, many potential hazards can be avoided but, as stated earlier, you must also keep the subject at the forefront of your thoughts whenever you are handling a shotgun or ammunition. *Think Safe — Be Safe.*

Such exhortations may be heeded by the newcomer to the sport but, in writing the preceding paragraphs, I am conscious that many veterans will skip over them, comfortable in the knowledge that they have never caused a shooting accident and, hence, have nothing to learn. At the risk of offending such worthies I would beg to be permitted to assure them that the contempt bred of familiarity is especially dangerous when applied to shotguns and shooting. By no means all tragedies result from the bunglings of the inexperienced, and should any reader feel that this chapter smacks of teaching granny to suck eggs, might I humbly suggest that one life is worth an awful lot of egg-sucking.

Natural Hazards

In theory, all risks arising from the simple use of shotguns should be avoidable. In coastal wildfowling, however, there are other hazards which are of a different nature entirely. An observer from another galaxy might be forgiven for thinking man to be a very strange creature in that he appears to deliberately place himself in danger purely, it might seem, for the purpose of gaining some perverse satisfaction from using his skills to overcome those self-imposed risks. Motor racing, hang gliding and mountaineering are prime examples, but there are many other sporting and leisure activities which, to a greater or lesser extent, provide similar challenges and thrills. Because wildfowling is carried out in difficult terrain, amid oozing mud and racing tides, with the uncertainty of winter weather always present, there are inevitably many situations in which disaster might be the consequence of a misjudgement or ill-considered action.

Whereas it might be exhilarating to face danger and survive, there is a world of difference between courage and foolhardiness. The wildfowler not only must be completely aware of the hazards which he might encounter, he needs to know the limitations of his information and equipment and, most of all, he must know when to call a halt to his expedition. It is no comfort to a widow to know that she lost her husband because the weather forecast was inaccurate or the tide flowed an hour before time. Nor will her grief be lessened by the knowledge that his death resulted from a faulty boat rather than from an error of judgement on the part of the deceased fowler.

Conditions on the foreshore can change dramatically and suddenly, each locality having its own individual characteristics and foibles. Whereas it was possible to lay down ground rules governing the handling of shotguns, it is not feasible to eliminate all possibility of accidents from other causes quite so readily. There is a measure of advice which can have fairly universal application and certain fundamental principles will form the basis of each wildfowler's knowledge. Experience cannot be built up overnight, however, and each sportsman must tread with the utmost caution until he has come to terms with the quirks of his local estuary.

Drowning and exposure are the most serious consequences of misadventure on the marsh, as newspaper headlines such as 'Wash Claims Another Victim' or 'Three Men in a Boat Lost on Tay' testify with tragic regularity. The latter faced me as I wrote the first edition of this book and the story appeared to be that, in the middle of a prolonged period of extremely cold weather, three fowlers set out by dinghy to reach Mugdrum Island in the Firth of Tay. That island can provide prime sport in such conditions but the three hapless sportsmen never reached their destination. So cold had the weather been that the estuary was full of pack ice which had drifted down-river. Unfortunately small rowing boats are not designed to withstand an encounter with ice floes and all three wildfowlers perished.

The north shore of the Tay estuary can be a very dangerous place in winter.

I did not personally know the three men who lost their lives on that occasion but, as I commenced the planning of this revised edition of *Modern Wildfowling*, I was stunned to learn that a friend who had assisted with many BASC projects in the Fife and Tayside areas had been drowned on the very first day of the season. There was no ice involved in this accident; merely a sudden deterioration in the weather which resulted in heavy waves on the Tay estuary. The small boat in which three fowlers were returning from morning flight broke up in the heaving sea and, although two men reached the shore, the third drowned. In this case there was no question of the victim being inexperienced or reckless. He was a very skilful fowler of many years standing and had made the same boat journey countless times.

Tides

Traditionally the threat of being overtaken or cut off by an advancing tide has been regarded as the principal danger faced by the coastal wildfowler. Particularly on expansive saltings there is a tendency to underestimate the speed of the tidal flow and it must be borne in mind constantly that the flatter the marsh, the greater the race of incoming water. Neither should the combined effect of wind and tide be forgotten. It seems likely that more novices get into difficulty by slavishly believing the published tide tables than by ignoring them altogether. A gale from offshore can bring the time of high tide forward by a full hour and raise its height by several feet. You must, therefore, not only have your route back to the sea wall charted in advance, you must also be prepared to take it earlier than planned in the event of any abnormal circumstances arising.

Mud and Fog

Retreating in front of an advancing tide is a hair-raising experience at the best of times but the unfortunate fowler is liable to have his problems compounded by additional factors such as mud or fog which stack the odds heavily against him. Plowtering through the ooze of a tidal estuary is a skill in itself and many a boot has been lost as a result of inexperience in the art. The secret is to be deliberate yet gentle in every movement, to develop a rhythm and to apply a little thought to each sequence of steps. I rather imagine that those folk who are expert ballroom dancers will also find themselves to be particularly sure-footed in the mud. The panic stricken fowler attempting to beat an incoming tide is not in the best position to learn the secrets of such a delicate form of locomotion.

Fog is another hazard which can cause sufficient difficulty on its own without meeting it in circumstances which are already fraught with danger. A rolling grey mantle can engulf the entire marsh in a matter of minutes and the wildfowler who does not know his bearings will find himself in real trouble. Whereas the man who is safely ensconced above high water mark has the option of sitting tight until conditions improve, his colleague out on the saltings will be forced to move and, in the absence of known land-marks, runs the risk of becoming well and truly lost.

Risk to Life and Limb

Other dangers which confront the longshore gunner are the possibility of falling and breaking a leg or ankle, a host of problems which can arise as a result of taking to the water in inadequate craft and risks to health which might follow a sojourn on the winter foreshore while inadequately dressed.

The latter two categories can be readily avoided by careful advance planning but the chance of becoming immobilised as the result of a fall is always present and only exceptional care can reduce the risk.

What a gloomy picture I seem to have painted! In fact, I have felt really scared only twice while wildfowling and on both occasions there was no real danger of anything worse than discomfort once the correct course of action had been established. Many years ago, while shooting early season duck on the Forth estuary, I persuaded a friend to take his small rowing boat out to an island in the Firth near Alloa. While we were engrossed in flighting mallard and teal, the wind rose to a degree which made a return to the shore impossible. The realisation of our position was accompanied by considerable dismay but more rational thought soon prevailed and we sought out a sheltered spot in which to wait. Within a few hours the gale abated and allowed us to row to safety. Had we been on an island or mudbank which became covered by the high tide, then our plight would have been rather more precarious.

On the second occasion, while negotiating a particularly soft area of the Eden estuary, I made the mistake of halting to take a shot at a single pintail drake which ventured within range. The pause in my progress through the mud was sufficient to trap both feet and, try as I might, I could do nothing to free my waders from the suction which held them tight. A brief moment of panic arose as I pictured my entire person being swallowed up by the black ooze but it was only a matter of seconds before the survival programme was whirring through my mental computer and the realities of the situation began to take shape. Pull feet out of waders — roll over half a turn — bring up knees — on to feet — and now keep moving. The cost of a new pair of thigh boots amounted to rather less of a loss than had been envisaged in those first few moments of fear. Had I not missed the pintail, it might almost have been worthwhile.

Two mishaps in many hundreds of days wildfowling may not suggest that we are engaged in a particularly perilous pastime but, as in all matters concerning safety, it pays always to err firmly on the side of caution.

Promoting Safety

To avoid becoming a statistic in the accident records should be our constant aim and this is best achieved by systematic attention to what the statisticians might term 'probability reduction'. Put simply, we must take every precaution which is open to us and use our skill and knowledge to prevent hazardous situations arising. A positive mental attitude to safety is essential and we must be critically aware of our own limitations. In addition, there are a number of systematic steps which we can take to promote safety on the shore.

Reconnaissance

The very first priority must be to build up an intimate and comprehensive understanding of the conditions of the estuary or marsh. Summer days spent on the shore, exploring every gully, channel and creek will acquaint the fowler with the topography of his local area together with the pattern of normal tides. Of particular value will be a knowledge of the order in which the various channels fill up with the tide and, hence, the parts of the marsh which present the greatest danger of becoming cut off from dry land. Areas of dangerously soft mud can be mentally charted and escape routes of firmer shingle noted. The summer wildlife of the locality will differ markedly from that encountered during the shooting season and hunting those species with a camera provides an intriguing warm weather hobby which supplies an excuse for being on the shore in daylight. We do get storms in spring and summer and, whenever possible, advantage should be taken of gale conditions. When the meteorological reports indicate a wild, windy day, the novice wildfowler will learn much by spending a few hours simply observing the effect of high winds on the tides of his estuary.

When visiting a strange area for a wildfowling expedition it may not always be possible to carry out a thorough daytime reconnaissance. In this event the wildfowler must be doubly careful and is well advised to stay close to the sea wall or, alternatively, seek out a trustworthy local guide. Large-scale maps can be useful for advance planning but it is imperative that the most up-to-date edition be used as foreshore areas are subject to comparatively rapid change as the natural processes of silting and erosion take place.

Forecasts

The second prerequisite of any peregrination beyond high water mark is to be thoroughly familiar with the weather and tide forecasts. As mentioned earlier, both are liable to be less than wholly accurate and the wildfowler requires to know how to judge the factors which may influence them. Once again, there is no ready alternative to experience which can only be gained season by season. The published and broadcast data will be the best guide available to the newcomer to the sport. Until such time as his battery of references has been developed, any dramatic deterioration in the weather must be taken as the cue to move to firmer ground. Although the very best wildfowling is to be obtained in really foul conditions, the foreshore debutant should not fear that advice of the sort given above necessarily excludes him from prime sport. When a gale is howling and dark storm clouds scud across the dawn sky there is really no need to venture far beyond the sanctuary of the sea wall as, on such mornings, excellent flighting may frequently be obtained from the reed fringes.

Equipment

In addition to reconnaissance and planning, equipment can play a vital part in promoting safety on the saltings. One item which every book recommends is a good, reliable compass. A compass is undoubtedly an essential part of the wildfowler's kit but it is of limited value unless one knows how to use it. The cardinal rule, especially on a strange estuary, is to take frequent compass bearings when walking out to the edge of the marsh. If a thick swirling fog suddenly descends, the magnetic needle will give no useful information if the fowler does not know the direction in which he must travel to reach the sea wall. The time to consult your compass, therefore, is before setting out from the sea wall and, again, when you reach your chosen flighting position. The best possible plan is to use a sunny Sunday afternoon to prepare a personal chart of your local estuary, marking in all the topographical hazards and taking compass bearings for the safe routes to the sea wall. Seal your chart into polythene and carry it with you whenever you go out with gun and dog.

Another useful tip is always to carry a wading stick. This need not add much weight to the fowler's load and a light aluminium or alloy pole, painted matt brown, will enable mud or water to be tested for depth without risking a bootful of icy brine. A stick also aids balance when traversing soft ground and, if you have the flight of a lifetime, a couple of dozen duck can be tied to it for the return journey over the marsh.

If a fowler does have to spend a long time in adverse conditions waiting for a tide to turn or for thick fog to lift, his comfort and his health will be greatly helped by a Thermos flask of hot tea or coffee. I know that it is tempting to travel as light as is possible but a hot drink could be a lifesaver on the estuary and it is well worth including a flask in your bag as a matter of course.

Many of the problems which wildfowlers face arise from being out on a midwinter estuary before dawn or after dusk. While every good book will caution against the indiscriminate use of a torch during the hours of darkness, there are times when, for safety's sake, one should be carried. The problem is that most of the pocket torches on the market are worse than useless when the chips are down. The only realistic answer is to opt for either a large heavy-duty handlamp or one of the ultra-light, high intensity torches. If carrying a bit of extra weight is not a hindrance, then I really would recommend the Ever Ready model 5800 Powerbeam hand-lamp. It takes two of the large PJ996 batteries (which accounts for the weight) but it does throw a really powerful beam and can be relied upon to give many years of hard service. The alternative is a truly pocketable lamp of the type which throws a high-intensity beam and the best I have found so far is the Mini-Maglite which is imported from the USA and comes in a complete kit including a lanyard and coloured signalling lenses. The lanyard is handy and you will, of course, need the batteries in the kit but you can throw the rest away. The beauty of this product is that it can sit in the bottom of a coat pocket and be virtually unnoticed until it is required. The light given out is really remarkable for the size of the torch and, provided that it is not used much, may be just what is required in an emergency.

Please try not to use a torch at all when making your way over the saltings before morning flight. Your eyes should grow accustomed to the darkness quite quickly and it is rare for the night to be so black that you cannot make progress safely. A torch is handy, however, if you have to get out of a tricky situation quickly or for helping you to gather up your belongings after an evening flight. Most of all, however, it should be regarded as a signalling device in the event that you hit real trouble.

An immediate concern of the fowler who gets cut off by the tide or lost in fog is to attempt to summon help. Traditionally the accepted alarm signal was to fire three shots in quick succession, but I fear that shooting pressure on some coasts is now so great that such a signal would go unnoticed amongst the barrage of fire which can be heard on a busy Saturday morning. Nevertheless, a situation of potential disaster is no time to conserve cartridges so fire them off anyway and hope that someone takes notice. In any case, if you have to resort to swimming across a flooded creek, you will not be assisted by the weight of a full box of shells. In clear weather it may be possible to attract attention by tying a white cloth to the wading stick and using it as a flag while, if fog descends in fairly still conditions, a loud whistle may be heard over a fairly long distance. Unfortunately the type which most of us use for gundog work is unlikely to give the piercing blast which will guide a rescue party to the spot where we are stranded with a broken leg, but specialist safety whistles are readily available. The best known range is probably the various Acme models produced by J Hudson & Co. Ltd. in Birmingham. Their plastic Model 649 air/sea rescue whistle is ideal for the wildfowler as it is not affected by submersion in sea water. Like the Mini-Maglite torch, a whistle of this type can remain in the coat pocket until an emergency arises and the fowler will notice neither the weight nor the bulk.

Another invaluable accessory is the Tidemaster Quartz Chronometer which is a very serviceable and accurate wristwatch ideally suited to the wildfowler. In a smart black rubber casing, it is waterproof and shock-resistant but its main additional feature is a special bezel around the perimeter of the watch face. By setting the bezel to the correct time for either high or low tide (from your tide tables or a phone call to the local harbourmaster), the watch will then tell you the current state of the tide throughout the following twelve hours.

Boats

Finally, a word about boats. Although I fancied myself as an estuarine sailor at one stage of my wildfowling career, I must now confess to having some sympathy with those fowlers who regard rowing dinghies as a sign of greed on the overpopulated foreshores of the present day. Circumstances vary from place to place but on some estuaries it is undoubtedly the case that one wildfowler who sets himself afloat may ruin the flight for a dozen who are waiting at the sea wall. If, however, you have a legitimate need for a boat — to reach an island perhaps — please ensure that it is sufficiently substantial for the task in hand and that it has been carefully maintained throughout the close season.

Although I have never lost any wildfowling friends as a result of them being drowned after becoming cut off by the tide or in consequence of them being swallowed up by treacherous mud, I have — as mentioned earlier — lost one because of an incident involving a boat for fowling.

One sensible precaution would be to make a point of always wearing a lifejacket whenever using a boat. Furthermore, the gun should always be kept in its sleeve while travelling afloat and it is important to remember that it is illegal to shoot from a boat while it is under power.

Conclusion

A cardinal rule, related to safety, is always to leave word at home or in your hotel so that someone knows where you are and when you are expected to return. It will aid the rescue services immeasurably if they know where to start looking.

So there we have it — desperate to take ourselves out on to the marsh, but apparently weighted down by a positive plethora of dos and don'ts, any breach of which will put us in mortal danger. Let me repeat that safety is an attitude of mind. We must always think in terms of potential hazards and act so as to minimalise the risk. The competent wildfowler will be constantly aware of the weather, tide and ground conditions but enjoys himself all the more because he has taken on nature on her own terms and proved himself equal to the challenge. Whatever risks he may encounter, he will gain enormous satisfaction from the knowledge that he has them sussed out and summed up. Safety on the shore is an attitude of mind. *Think Safe — Be Safe*.

9

Flightcraft

Each wildfowling season is different and provides a unique set of circumstances which will determine the type of sport which a fowler may enjoy. A few years ago I remember becoming increasingly frustrated because it seemed that the conditions would never be right for a flight under the moon. With each successive full moon we watched the sky hopefully; searching for the conditions which can spell success on the saltings. In October and November the skies were too clear. The ideal conditions for a moonflight occur when a thin veil of cloud masks the full moon and provides a light backdrop against which any ducks or geese will be silhouetted. A cloudless sky is inky black and, under such circumstances, birds will be heard but not seen. December was even worse. The full moon just before Christmas was accompanied by thick rain-clouds which darkened the sky and made shooting impossible. Such are the disappointments of the coastal wildfowler.

We thought that January was also going to be a washout. Heavy cloud cover marred most of the full moon period and it seemed that the entire season might pass without a single opportunity to do business with the nightflighting fowl. Then, two days after the full moon, I was just preparing to climb into bed when Tom phoned. 'Look out your window', he instructed. I did — and saw nothing. 'The moon is perfect for a flight,' he added. 'Are you coming out?'

I should explain that Tom lives almost on the estuary, while my own home is thirty miles to the west. Although my pal was reporting perfect cloud conditions at the coast, the sky above me was still dark with thick clouds and, indeed, rain was falling. The chance was not one to be missed, however, and I told Tom I would meet him at the old railway crossing in forty minutes. My wife took one look at the clock — it was half-past midnight — and told me that I was completely mad! Although I was inclined to agree, I proceeded to gather together gun, cartridges and waterproofs before releasing the old labrador from her kennel and setting off along the A91 towards St Andrews.

Passing into Kinross-shire the rain ceased and, as the Fife border was reached, the clouds thinned and the faint orb of the moon shone through them. By the time I met Tom, above the estuary, conditions seemed perfect, although there was no guarantee that they would remain that way. The tide was well out so we crawled along the river channel for almost a mile before finding a place to hide. Waders piped their plaintive tunes as we disturbed them but, as yet, we had heard nothing of the wigeon or pinkfeet which we hoped would be flighting under the moon.

As we settled into our gullies a small pack of duck circled around, low and fast. My gun went up and, just in time, their wingbeats identified them as shelduck. I don't know how often I have been saved from committing that particular crime just in the nick of time. A single quack then broke the silence and Tom's gun spoke once, bringing a fat mallard duck tumbling to the mud.

That was the extent of the action for almost an hour and we were beginning to feel the night chill creeping through our thermals when the beloved calling of pinkfooted geese pervaded the night sky. The birds must have been roosting in the inner basin and, finally, had decided that the silvery moonlight was sufficiently bright to let them indulge in a nocturnal nosh-up. Needless to say, those pinks headed straight off the saltings without coming anywhere near our position. Their departure did, however, signal the start of a more general level of activity throughout the estuary. Small groups of pinkfeet flighted in from the outer sands and wigeon traversed the marsh, searching for the most succulent grazing.

By the time that Tom and I called it a day (or a night) at 4.30 a.m., we had accounted for only one mallard, one pinkfoot and three wigeon but, as a last-gasp attempt at moonflighting, it was highly fulfilling. Although there may be only a few nights each season when conditions are right, fowling under the moon is an incredibly satisfying experience.

Flighting Behaviour

Shooting geese and duck under the moon is just one method of coming to terms with the quarry. Morning and evening flights are more common while tide flighting can, under the correct conditions, also be a fruitful strategy. All of those activities do, however, require that the wildfowler understands the behaviour of the birds which he hunts. Having considered the quarry species and the guns, clothing and equipment which will assist the estuarine wildfowler to pursue them effectively and safely, it is now appropriate to turn our attention to the ways and means of arranging an assignation with the fowl of the shore.

It is well known that duck roost on the marsh or on open water by day, flighting inland to feed at dusk, while their larger cousins, the wild geese, reverse the process and roost by night, flying off the foreshore at dawn to graze on agricultural land or pasture. Or at least they sometimes do. In fact, while geese normally follow a fairly regular pattern, only deviating from their routine when foul weather, undue disturbance or a full moon occurs, duck are considerably less predictable and one frequently wonders if they have read the correct instruction manuals.

With the exception of flight pond shooting, most wildfowling is dependent upon calculating the flightlines of the duck and geese and lying in wait to ambush them as they fly past. Whereas in the 'bad old days' of Hawker it was common to adopt stalking practices using horses or cattle as mobile blinds or, more usually, to take advantage of the natural gutters and creeks to get within gunshot range of resting fowl, such schemes are nowadays impracticable or would be considered unsporting on the foreshores of modern Britain. A large part of marshcraft, therefore, lies in developing the skill to predict where the quarry will fly within range of a waiting gun.

Greylag geese are not averse to spending the night afloat.

Geese

As they present a less complex case, let us first consider the factors which can help us to intercept geese. As stated previously, the longshore gunner should normally flight geese only in the morning so as to avoid the danger of disturbing the roost. There are places where an evening flight can be both profitable and harmless but, until he gets to know his goose grounds, the novice is well advised to stick to the general rule. Conditions vary on different estuaries but, by and large, grey geese spend the hours of darkness at rest and favour places which offer calm conditions and security.

Where there are sandbanks a few hundred yards offshore these will frequently be used and geese generally are not averse to spending part of the night on water where the banks are covered at high tide. Indeed, on inland lochs it is normal for the birds to spend the entire roost period afloat. In locations where the uncovered foreshore extends sufficiently far from the sea wall to offer reasonable safety, geese will often roost at the tide's edge, taking to the water when the incoming flow pushes them too close to civilisation.

Effect of Wind and Weather

As a major difficulty facing the shore-based wildfowler is the height at which geese habitually fly over the sea wall, there is considerable benefit in knowing the conditions which are likely to bring them lower. Not only do storm force winds tend to compel the birds to fly at lesser altitudes, such weather also makes roosting on open water less comfortable. By selecting a windy morning when the tide will be approaching full at around the time of dawn, a fowler can draw additional advantage from the likelihood that the starting point for the flight will be closer to the high water mark than is normally the case.

The timing of morning flight is likewise subject to considerable variation and the experienced wildfowler should be able to make an educated guess at both the time and duration in different conditions. On a calm, relatively cloud-free morning geese may flight from their roosting areas at any time between one hour before sunrise and one hour after. Dirty weather will delay the lightening of the sky and may consequently postpone the movement of the birds. If, however, tide conditions are pressing, high winds may cause them to flight earlier to avoid sitting on choppy seas. All other things being equal, geese which are resting on the salt marsh may flight earlier when being inched along by an incoming tide than they would during the ebb.

Hungry birds are clearly more likely to leave the roost earlier than normal and this factor may be important in times of food shortage, such as occurs when there is general snow cover on the fields at sea level. Conversely, during periods of the full moon geese may feed during the night and, as a result, be less pressed by hunger pangs in the morning. It is at the full moon that the flock movements are least predictable and the fowler planning a visit to a distant estuary is wise to avoid such times when selecting the dates for his holiday.

A final point in relation to the effects of wind, weather and tides on goose behaviour is that on calm nights, when the tide is well out just prior to dawn, geese tend to congregate in large roosting flocks on the water or on the open marsh. Under such conditions they will frequently flight in huge skeins of up to 300 birds and the fowler who happens to lie underneath them may thrill to the sight of so many geese but, once they have passed, he is unlikely to get a second chance that morning. On the other hand, when the elements are approaching storm level and the tide is well advanced at flight time, the fowl are apt to be found in smaller, scattered groups, each of which will flight separately over an extended period and may provide the waiting wildfowler with a number of sporting chances.

Duck

Attempting to apply a similar analysis to the factors governing the movement of duck is somewhat less fruitful on account of the more complicated behaviour patterns of the smaller birds. While it is true that for most of the shooting season the major quarry duck species will roost by day and feed by night, the roosting sites and feeding areas are by no means constant. Additionally, young juvenile duck, on occasion, reverse the common pattern and, under some circumstances, adult duck will move about during the daylight hours.

Mallard may roost on an estuary and flight inland at dusk to feed on flooded barley stubbles or a shallow pond. Wigeon may spend the day at rest on a large inland lake and move out to the salt marsh to feed on *zostera* at night. Pintail sometimes pass the day at the mouth of a river and flight upstream in the evening. Although it is reasonably certain that duck activity will be greatest during the hours around sunrise and sunset, the unfortunate fowler commonly finds them moving in both directions simultaneously.

Generally speaking, duck flight in poorer light than geese so that the morning wildfowler must expect them earlier. This is a perpetual problem to fowlers on estuaries where both geese and duck may be encountered as there is a great temptation to shoot at a mallard which is heading out, replete after a night on the potato fields, and risk disturbing the geese which may be roosting only a few hundred yards away. In most localities etiquette demands that the duck be spared under such circumstances. It is, I am afraid, one of those situations in which Murphy's Law inevitably applies — if you shoot at the duck, all the geese will take to the air at the sound of the shot and head in the opposite direction; if you let the duck pass unsaluted, the geese will be undisturbed, you will wait expectantly for another hour, and then they will fly in the opposite direction anyway!

Evening Flight

Evening is the real time to go in search of duck and the prudent sportsman can greatly increase his success rate by careful study of the topography of the region and the roosting and feeding sites of the duck which inhabit it. Daylight reconnaissance will show the offshore roosts of the birds and also the probable inland feeding places. Droppings and feathers are only a reliable indicator in this context if the fowler is competent to assess their age. The knowledge that duck frequently follow natural watercourses can be used to predict likely routes which will be taken and thus possible interception points planned.

Another fruitful time for flighting duck is when the tide is flowing over the saltings by day. Birds which are loafing and preening on the flats will move back and forward as the incoming water covers their favoured sites, affording sporting shooting to the knowledgeable fowler who has observed their behaviour on previous occasions. The secret is to choose a hide position past which the duck will fly before the position itself is flooded by the tide. On a strange marsh, tide-flighting can be a useful way of becoming familiar with the terrain before venturing out in darkness.

Driftwood and flotsam can provide an effective hide.

Concealment

Whatever the quarry, and irrespective of whether it is sought at dawn, dusk or mid-day, the novice wildfowler must learn how to conceal himself on the marsh so as to remain unnoticed by the duck or geese until they are within range of his armament. The wariness of wildfowl is quite incredible and, especially in areas where shooting pressure is heavy, they become astonishingly adept at spotting a human form ensconced on the shore. Attention to clothing is important and, in addition to utilising garments which blend into the background, it is vital to ensure that there are no bright metal buttons or buckles which might flash in the light of the rising or setting sun.

Natural camouflage should be used as much as possible and, when flighting close to the sea wall, it is often a simple matter to throw together a hide from the flotsam and seaweed which litters the high water mark. Artificial hides using army surplus netting, collapsible poles and suchlike are useful in some situations but it is essential that they blend into the natural landscape. A green and brown camouflage net is worse than useless when erected against the pale straw-coloured backdrop of January reed-beds. My own favourite material is the matt PVC 'Leafscreen' which is available in both green and straw shades. It is extremely light to carry, takes up little space in the bag and, perhaps most importantly, it is virtually tangle-free. This latter quality is a real boon when attempting to erect a hide in the darkness. A man-made hide, whether of a temporary or permanent nature, will be less obvious if constructed against some natural feature such as a washed-up tree trunk, an eroded banking or a stony scree.

Where possible, build a hide against a natural feature such as this banking.

Irrespective of the form of hide or the materials from which it is built, the cardinal rule is that it must not be silhouetted against the sky when seen from the direction from which the quarry will approach. In suitable locations a permanent hide has the advantage that it can be left unused until the duck and geese have become accustomed to it and, additionally, it can be made more comfortable than a temporary erection. Where circumstances do permit the building of this type of hide, the wildfowler will find that timber pallets are exceptionally useful as they are not only strong and conveniently sized but, being hollow, they can be filled with soil and mud to weigh them down and to provide a substrate for the growth of grasses and other vegetation in future years.

It is not always possible, of course, to have the comparative luxury of a hide from which to shoot. Much of the time it is incumbent upon the fowler to conceal himself as best he can by using such areas of shade and small protuberances as might exist upon the shore. In this event it is vital to get as low as can be arranged and it is worth bearing in mind that the human form is often less obvious when crouched in front of a dark backdrop than when peering over the top of it. Many experienced fowlers insist that a face veil is necessary in this type of situation but, personally, I prefer to rely on the wide peak of a suitable hat casting a shadow over my face.

Whether snug in a hide, uncomfortably crouched in a damp gutter or merely attempting to be invisible in a bed of seaweed on an otherwise featureless shore, try to avoid moving once you are in position. The slight movement of a fowler's head turning to survey an arc of 180° will be sufficient to flash warning signals to any bird which might be approaching. The kind of shifty side-to-side glance which is associated with dubious characters in second-rate detective films is absolutely ideal on the foreshore as the more of the panorama you can cover by eye movement alone, the less chance there will be of spooking the quarry.

Cover may often be found in the reed fringes of an estuary.

Sight and Sound

Apart from knowing where to hide and how to ensure reasonable concealment, there are other skills which must be learned by the apprentice fowler. Many of these will be acquired only as a result of hard experience but others can be taught by a good companion. This is one of the fundamental reasons for becoming a member of a wildfowling club — after you have been accepted by the local veterans you will have access to a wealth of knowledge concerning the features and idiosyncrasies of your principal fowling grounds.

Because much wildfowling takes place at dawn or dusk, there can be vision problems to be overcome and the selection of a hide site must take these into account. In poor light, duck can virtually disappear against a dark background and there is nothing more frustrating than to follow the aproach of birds in an open sky, only to lose them against trees or hills on the opposite side of the estuary just as they are coming into range. Similarly, in conditions of near darkness, duck or geese may be clearly visible when silhouetted against a background of fairly light cloud but will not readily be picked up in the inky black of a cloudless sky.

At morning flight these problems are less acute as the strengthening light improves as each minute passes. It is a very different story at dusk, however, as the accommodation of the eyes to the growing darkness always lags slightly behind the ideal state. In the evening, therefore, it is desirable to arrange one's position so that incoming fowl will be seen against what remains of the light in the western sky.

When beset by such difficulties the wildfowler rapidly learns to use his ears as well as his eyes, and before long he may well rely upon hearing to pinpoint the direction of approach of duck and geese in the seconds before they become visible. With experience he will find that he not only knows the point at which his eyes will pick up the bird, but also that he has identified it before it comes into view. This is one crucial reason for taking every possible step to protect the vital sense of hearing from damage due to over-exposure to gunshot blasts. A further aid in inadequate light is a good dog which will usually detect quarry at a considerably greater distance than will its handler. Indeed, there have been evenings when I have given up searching the darkening sky for duck and simply watched my labrador. The old dog inevitably gives sufficient warning for a shot to be obtained when frequently the bird would have been past and gone, had I relied upon my own senses.

Inland Waters

Although this book is concerned primarily with the form of wildfowling that can only take place in the truly wild conditions of an estuary, tidal foreshore or salt marsh, I will deviate briefly to spend a little time considering inland duck flighting. This I do in order to introduce the subject of decoys, as their main use is on the inland lake or small flight pond.

I shall refrain from subjecting the reader to another bombardment of my views on the abominable practice of shooting semi-tame mallard on oversized goldfish pools. There are, I must admit, more sporting forms of inland duck shooting which require a fair degree of skill and fieldmanship and it is with these that I shall dally for a moment.

We know that duck may roost on expansive inland waters in just the same manner as they do on the sea and, in such instances, they may be flighted coming into the lake in the morning or leaving it in the evening. As the shooting on these waters is not public, any sportsman who rents a shoot which contains or adjoins a large water can build permanent hides in the most likely places. The points at which streams enter or leave the lake are probable hide sites, as are patches of dense reeds or rushes. The prudent Shot will not overshoot such a resource and will try to ensure that it remains relatively undisturbed so that wildfowl might adopt it as a regular home.

An inland duck shoot of this type has one great advantage when compared to the open foreshore and that is the opportunity which exists to undertake improvement work to enhance the water both as a duck habitat and as a place which will provide exciting sport. In a later chapter I shall describe some of the conservation principles which can make a lake more attractive to fowl and I have already mentioned the possibility of constructing permanent hides of butts. At one time I tenanted the shooting on Loch Fitty, a 160-acre loch in Fife, and being fairly proud of the facilities which existed there I invited WAGBI (as the BASC then was) to base a wildfowling and conservation course on the water. One of the guest lecturers was that great fowling author, Arthur Cadman, and I was amazed at the vast list of improvements which he was able to suggest for the loch. Since that day I have tended to regard every wetland situation as a potential duck shoot, if only time and energy could be made available to undertake the blasting, digging, planting and building which might be necessary.

Decoys

To reduce the element of chance which exists in such shooting, it may be desirable to employ decoys to draw incoming duck to within range of the guns. After all, if there are hundreds of acres of water available, why should the fowl choose to land in any particular area? In the United States of America decoy-carving is a highly developed art and, together with duck calling, has become a competitive activity and sport in its own right. In this country less attention has been paid to the subject and the majority of shooting men are content to purchase rubber duck from their gun and tackle retailer. Many of those commercial products are far too glossy and, as

Mallard decoy and call.

the merest hint of shine will chase wildfowl into the next county, they require to be rubbed down to a matt finish before use. Most, too, could profitably be larger so as to catch the attention of airborne fowl at greater distances.

Decoys must adopt a natural 'swim' when placed on the water, movement and aspect being far more important than accurate colouring. The type which has a weighted keel seems superior in this respect. In general terms, the greater the number of decoys used, the more effective will they be. Avoid, however, a very regular pattern of rubber mallard in regimented rows. While it is true that duck usually sit facing the wind, they rarely do so in neat lines. When setting out the decoys it is wise to remember that duck normally come in to land into the wind and the gunner should position himself and his flotilla with this in mind.

The other type of inland duck shooting which is often undertaken at the end of a day's roughshooting is to wait for the birds at evening by the side of a small flight pond. Almost any little area of water can be made to attract duck if it provides worthwhile feeding, and on many shoots suitable ponds or flood flashes are regularly fed with barley, other grain or waste fruit and potatoes. I was once a member of a shoot where the gamekeeper's wife ran a fruit shop and the keeper frequently made an early morning visit to the fruit market in Glasgow. One year a dock strike resulted in huge quantities of over-ripe bananas being available to anyone who wished to transport them away and we enjoyed sport at the flight pond that season such as had never been experienced previously. The only qualification which I would make about this type of sport is that the duck must be wild birds which have come from the sea or a nearby lake. Inland sport in the gloaming hour is not worth turning out for if the duck are tame, incautious and poor fliers.

It is very important to avoid overshooting a flight pond but, in suitable circumstances, between six and eight flights per season might be possible. In the evening decoys are less effective as the failing light reduces their attracting powers. A well-fed pond which is left undisturbed will have a regular clientele of mallard and teal but it may still be worthwhile putting down a few decoys to give the early arrivals confidence and draw the duck to the desired end of the water.

Decoys on the Estuary

Having introduced the topic of duck decoys by relating them to their more common uses on inland waters and flight ponds, let me now revert to the estuary and consider whether they might be of any benefit below the sea wall. At morning or evening flight the answer is probably in the negative. At these times the fowl know where they are going and have no thoughts of gatecrashing another party. When tide-flighting, on the other hand, there can be a degree of advantage derived from a set of judiciously placed decoys. When an incoming tide is moving duck over the saltings, they will normally seek a resting place which offers security and at least a few minutes respite from the advancing waves. By selecting a flash or pool on the marsh which appears to offer those features and by putting out some decoy duck, it may be possible to persuade the wildfowl that it is worth dropping in for a visit.

Calling

Related to the subject of decoying is that of calling wild duck and geese. Certain fowlers possess a real talent for imitating the calls of birds and can develop an uncanny skill in this respect. Many contemporaries will have heard the late Kenzie Thorpe demonstrating his prowess at imitating the voices of an extensive range of wildfowl. Once again, however, the majority of sportsmen rely upon artificial devices to reproduce the sounds of their quarry and a wide range of calls are produced and marketed. My own personal favourites are those produced by the Olt company in the USA, some of which are specially tuned to match the calls of British goose species. Bearing in mind that the object of the exercise is to attract the appropriate bird to within gunshot range, it is obviously essential that the correct note is produced. Just as some fowlers are experts at producing call-notes by mouth, so too are other artists with artificial calls. Mal Kempson, who has achieved fame as one of Scotland's top wildfowling guides, is a real virtuoso with the goose call and I have often listened and watched in amazement as he has turned entire skeins of pinkfeet which appeared to be flighting on a set course.

Despite the fact that some fowlers become expert at calling, I rather fear that it is more common for the tyro to rush into his local sports shop,

End of a successful flight.

hurriedly exchange a few pound coins for a wooden call-whistle and then take to the shore blowing his new toy without first studying the natural sounds of the species he hopes to attract. The laws of chance would seem to predict that the likelihood of producing the correct sound is very small and the possibility of emitting a warning or alarm call is more probable than fortuitously quacking an attracting note. From this point of view, I really would recommend that the novice fowler invests in one of the excellent instructional audio cassettes which will tutor him in the use of his call.

Fieldcraft

At this point it is perhaps worth stressing that the purpose of attempting to develop a high level of competence at fieldcraft is to increase the frequency of sporting chances which present themselves and, thus, enhance the satisfaction which the fowler might derive from coming a little closer to being on equal terms with his quarry. Such equal terms will never, of course, be achieved but when a wildfowler becomes sufficiently proficient at his art, he ceases to be tempted to shoot at out-of-range birds or to take large bags on those occasions when hard weather makes the whole business unsporting. By being moderately successful some of the time, and appreciating the reasons for the empty bag the rest of the time, the foreshore fowler will find a contentment which can never be realised by the shooter who kills a dozen or more pinkfeet over decoys on an inland field. It is a sobering thought to realise that if one-third of all the Shotgun Certificate holders in Britain each killed one grey goose in a season, there would not be a single bird left to breed in the following year. Those who do pursue fowl have a heavy responsibility resting upon their shoulders.

It is also a sobering thought to appreciate that all the marvels of modern technology cannot significantly enhance the chances which a fowler has of successfully engaging his quarry. Or perhaps I jump to conclusions. Might it just be possible that we have been less inventive in relation to our sport than we have been in other areas of human endeavour? For example, surely it should be a practical proposition for an engineer with a little computer experience to devise a means of getting the wildfowler out of bed on the best mornings. A wind-speed indicator linked to a micro-computer which was programmed with tide times and moon phases should be able to sound an electronic alarm which would waken the fowler at the appropriate hour when a force-8 gale was brewing. Each year there are so few mornings when the optimum conditions occur that there can be real pain in rising from bed after sunrise to realise that the flight of the season has probably just ended.

10

The Fowler's Dog

'Did you hear the weather forecast?' asked Harry over the telephone lines. 'There's a real hurricane coming in from the Atlantic.' My pal Harry always was prone to a little exaggeration but I had seen the television weatherman looking somewhat worried as he pointed out the rapidly converging isobars on his chart and there seemed a good chance that the first gale of the winter was about to hit our shores. 'O.K. Harry' I replied, 'I'll pick you up at the crossroads at half past five and we'll head for Kingoodie.'

Sleep did not come readily as I lay awake fitfully listening to the rising wind battering the spiteful rain against my bedroom window. Finally, the alarm clock shrilled its cheerless reveille and I hastily donned thermal underwear and a warm woollen jersey. Breakfast and shaving were performed on automatic pilot and I was halfway across the yard to release the labradors from their kennel before the full force of the gale almost swept me from my feet.

Several times we had to stop the car and clear fallen branches from the roadway but, eventually, we reached the north shore of the Tay and drove east along the main Perth to Dundee road. The sodium lights of the city were beginning to add an orange tint to the night sky before we turned off the dual carriageway and crossed the railway line which runs parallel to the shore. That morning I reckoned that the weather would ensure that few other wildfowlers would be abroad. It's a funny thing, but many who claim to be fowlers just cannot get out of bed when the weather turns really nasty! I was right. As we pulled in to the familiar parking spot, there were no other vehicles to be seen. Hurriedly we tried to clamber into our waterproofs within the confines of the Volvo and, eventually, doors were opened and we stepped out into the teeth of the storm.

With Moy, Moss and Teal firmly in tow, a drunken path was followed down to the saltings and Harry elected to find cover in the sparse reed beds which had been virtually flattened by the wind. Picking my way cautiously over the rutted marsh, I finally gained the sanctuary of a deep creek and slid down to brave the elements and await the geese. For almost an hour I crouched, with the rain smashing into me, almost horizontally, before the sky lightened and the faint call of greylags could be heard above the howling of the gale.

When the great grey birds did flight, it was in classic style. They had clearly not relished remaining afloat on a gale-lashed sea and, accordingly, their starting point was closer to the sea wall than normal. With the wind in their tails, the great skeins sped along but, characteristically, they failed to gain height as they flipped over the foreshore. Harry was the first to score and I watched two birds tumble from a skein before the twin reports of his eight-bore boomed across the marsh. One of the benefits of fowling in such conditions is that the sound of gunshots is quickly lost amongst the general turmoil of the storm and the geese seem not to take undue notice of them.

Before long it was my turn. I crouched lower as the skein approached, trying to appear invisible to the beady eyes of the greylags. Suddenly they were above my creek and, before I could spring to my feet, the gale had whipped them out of range. 'Getting rusty in your old age!' I told myself, and a disgusted look from Moy added weight to the rebuke. The next group of greys passed right over Harry. He took a single bird from the skein and, at his shot, the birds swung around and headed for me. This time I made no mistakes and an ounce and a quarter of No. 3 shot flew from each barrel of the Beretta to find its mark.

Moy and Moss brought back a greylag apiece and I sank down against the muddy walls of my creek feeling exceedingly content. That really is the very spirit of wildfowling. A successful shot at wild geese in the wildest of weather. A million miles from civilisation and not a thought being given to the problems of the world. A warm glow as the labradors snuggle down beside the fowler and an all-pervading cosiness as the storm rages around. I was almost disappointed when Harry appeared at the edge of my creek and suggested that it was time to go home.

The Need for a Dog

That story emphasises the companionship which the fowler obtains from his gundog. There are times when the bond between man and dog is particularly intense but none more so than when sharing the solitude of the wild estuary. There is, however, another overwhelming reason for regarding a dog as being essential to coastal fowling. The deep regard in which the wildfowler holds his quarry is such that he will not deliberately fire a shot at any bird which may fall in a place from which it cannot be picked. It is axiomatic to the very nature of the sport that shots will present themselves when a duck or goose is flighting over a fast-flowing gully or an ebbing tide and, were the fowler to let all such chances pass him by, a very lean time might be had. To make the most of all the opportunities which arise, it is vital that a good retrieving dog is to hand.

During the years when I was an active participant in a nearby wild-fowling club, the most harrowing experiences I encountered seemed to arise from the attempts of some members to make do without a retriever. Indeed, one of my greatest triumphs was to finally persuade the club

Labradors make ideal wildfowling dogs.

chairman to invest in canine assistance after several seasons of dogless shooting.

At that time we regularly shot a fairly large and very wild inland loch. On a stormy morning — in strict accordance with Sod's Law — every duck shot would either fall in the waves or be blown thirty yards behind to drop in dense reed beds. Our chairman consistently managed to shoot more than his share of the rather sparse mallard population but most of his birds were fated to drift out of sight or lie unpicked in the rushes. Those of our number who possessed dogs grew angrier as the toll of lost birds mounted — not least because few duck flew over *our* positions — and finally an ultimatum was delivered to our colleague. Either he obtained a dog or he vacated his place in the shoot. It was with great pleasure that I subsequently received a telephone call asking for assistance in the construction of a kennel.

Choice of Breed

Whenever dogs are mentioned there inevitably arises a great debate concerning the virtues and attributes of the various breeds. Each has its band of devotees and each, no doubt, has its merits and demerits. To suggest that any particular variety of gundog is best suited to the sport of wildfowling is to invite immediate and violent reaction from all those fanciers of the others and it is, perhaps, less contentious merely to mention the qualities which should be sought in a dog which is primarily intended for service on the saltings.

First and foremost in this respect is the capability to take to near-freezing water and swim strongly. A hound which shirks this duty has no place by the fowler's side and certainly will bring him no credit. The ability to withstand severe cold is essential and on several occasions I have witnessed my own labradors emerge from the water on a winter morning and literally turn white with frost within a few minutes. Only a very hardy animal will absorb such deprivations and suffer no lasting ill effects, and yet so great is a gundog's love of the sport that it will happily leap into the coldest water again and again to retrieve shot birds.

Patience is another virtue which must be possessed by a dog which will be required to sit quietly by its handler's side for hours on end. A great many dogs would fail to meet this criterion yet be regarded as good rough-shooting gundogs. The hyperactivity which marks a gundog as a busy quester when seeking pheasant in a covert or partridge on a stubble is not a quality desired on the salt marsh. Personally I have always favoured labradors for wildfowling. Not only do they possess the above attributes in abundance; the breed normally displays an affability which I find appealing. There is little doubt, however, that the larger spaniels can equally stand up to the rigours of a January goose flight or that the other retriever breeds will acquit themselves well on the estuary.

Housing

The shooting man who is considering the acquisition of a canine companion must give some thought to the housing, health and feeding of his proposed charge. It seems almost natural to keep a dog in the house and, if treated thus, it will soon become part of the family. On the other hand, there are several weighty advantages to providing permanent quarters in a substantial outdoor kennel.

The hardiness which we seek in our dogs is more likely to be built up and maintained if they become accustomed to the extremes of climate as part of their day-to-day life. Furthermore, a dog which lives in a kennel will come to regard every training and exercise period as a real pleasure and will be keen to please its handler. Lastly, the outdoor dog is less likely to be spoiled by other members of the family who may find great difficulty in resisting the temptation to slip a tit-bit or two at mealtimes. There is little doubt that

A gundog will benefit from being housed in a substantial wooden kennel.

the dog which is handled by only one person will respond far more readily to training than will the confused creature which really does not know who to regard as the leader of the pack.

A labrador or springer spaniel will exist very happily in a wooden kennel measuring 6 feet wide by 4 feet deep by 4 feet high with a 6 feet by 6 feet run attached. Freedom from draughts and damp is essential and it is desirable to have a concrete slabbed base for the run area so that rainwater drains away quickly and the dog cannot dig itself out. For the kennel itself, overlapping weatherboard is probably the most suitable material but good quality exterior ply may be used as an alternative. A raised box will provide a suitable bed for the dog and, in winter, dry straw should be provided for bedding. In the summer months some owners prefer to give no bedding material in order to reduce the possibility of skin vermin being harboured.

Health and Feeding

Canine health is not normally a serious problem for the gundog owner as the mode of life of his dogs is infinitely healthier than that which the high-rise pooch enjoys in its centrally heated flat with a minimum of exercise around the concrete streets of a city. Nevertheless, it is essential that the wildfowler arranges for his puppy to be vaccinated against distemper, hardpad, jaundice, hepatitis and parvo-virus. A veterinary surgeon will readily give advice on this subject and will probably recommend booster vaccinations at annual intervals. The cost of such treatment is considerably lower than the loss of investment occasioned by the premature death of a good gundog or, indeed, the cost of curative medicine should the animal contract one of those ailments.

There are a number of steps which the wildfowler can take to ensure that his dog remains in good health. Plenty of exercise throughout the year is a prerequisite and care should be taken to avoid the dog becoming over-weight during the close season. Whereas I have mentioned the relish with which most gundogs will take to the water — even in near-freezing conditions — they will suffer if they are returned to their kennel after a midwinter swim without being thoroughly dried with a rough towel. The caring gundog owner will attend to his dog's need on arriving home from a wildfowling outing, giving this task priority even over the cleaning of his gun.

Feeding is a topic about which much has been written and about which dog owners will argue until the cows come home. In reality, it should not present any problem to the owner of only one or two dogs. A diet of raw meat or offal and coarse biscuit meal is perhaps the ultimate and allows the protein content to be maintained while the amount of carbohydrate is adjusted to meet the energy requirements of each individual dog, hence avoiding any tendency towards obesity. Far more convenient, however, are the all-in-one dog meals which are marketed in 20kg or 25kg sacks by a variety of reputable manufacturers. Some produce special formulations for active working dogs and most contain the necessary vitamins and mineral supplements.

It is normal to provide adult working dogs with only one meal each day but, after weaning, a puppy should be fed four or five times daily and the number of meals gradually reduced as the pup grows. I must confess that I personally prefer to maintain a feeding schedule of two meals per day right up until the dog's first birthday.

Purchasing a Puppy

Buying a gundog puppy can be a very chancy business and the wildfowler will do well to take every precaution which is available to him. Firstly, no dog should be considered which is not from proven working stock. There is really no need to buy a pup from the fellow round the corner when every issue of the weekly and monthly shooting periodicals carries a lengthy list of advertisements for litters which are Kennel Club registered and have field trial honours recorded on both sides of the family. Examination of the pedigree will also provide a warning against any excessive in-breeding.

It can be reassuring to see the dam working at the time of inspecting the puppies and even more encouraging if the youngsters are old enough to have begun basic training. A twelve week old puppy which will sit to command and come when called is likely to respond positively to further training. This is not always possible as many breeders prefer to sell their litters when the pups are seven or eight weeks old. On such occasions my personal, entirely unscientific rule is to choose the first pup of the desired sex which comes towards me when the litter is released.

Given that a gundog will cost in excess of £1,500 to feed and maintain during a normal canine lifetime, it really is crazy to try to save a few pounds at the time of buying a puppy. All of the hours spent training the dog will be wasted if it is not genetically predisposed to work in the field, and there is nothing more frustrating than realising that you have been lumbered

Gundog training equipment — dummy launcher, throwing dummy, feathered wing and staghorn whistle.

with a dog which will not respond to training and which will be a less than useful asset for a further twelve years or so. If the worst does happen, it is probably best to cut your losses before you become too attached to the dog, and pass it on to someone who wants nothing more than a family pet.

Training

Basic obedience training is the cornerstone upon which all further gundog work will be built and it is impossible to overemphasise the importance of the early lessons. This does not mean that a puppy should be denied its puppyhood. I have seen too many crazy mixed-up dogs which have suffered from over-zealous owners attempting to train too much too early.

Throughout training the golden rule is to praise the puppy enthusiastically every time it does something right. Psychologists call this 'response reinforcement' and such positive measures are clearly more effective than the old-style 'dog breaking'. Mild punishment can be administered *when absolutely necessary* by shaking the pup by the loose skin under the throat while administering a verbal scolding. Negative reinforcement of this type is *only* effective if it is applied *immediately* following the misdemeanour. The slightest delay can have unwanted effects. Perhaps the most obvious example of untimely punishment is to scold a dog for running away, once it has eventually returned. The dog associates the punishment with the action of returning rather than that of running away.

Use of Commands

At all stages of training, consistency is vital. This is particularly the case during the early months, and one of the first tasks of the handler is to select the words of command which will be used. There is a limit to the number of verbal stimuli to which a dog can reasonably be expected to respond, and the words should be chosen with care to ensure that they are not phonetically similar. My labradors have always been trained to obey the following signals:

Verbal:

Name	Used to summon the dog
Heel	Come to heel or walk to heel
Hup	Sit
Stay	Stay at sitting position
Down	Lie down
Hi-seek	Quest
Hi-lost	Find and Retrieve
Get-on	Move out in direction indicated by hand
Get-back	Move away from handler
Get-over	Jump fence of ditch
Kennel	Go to kennel

| No | Stop doing that |
| Leave-it | Put it down/do not pick it up |

Whistle:

One blast	Stop and sit
Two short blasts	Move towards handler
Repeated short blasts	Come to heel

Hand Signals:

Right hand raised	Stop and sit/stay
Hand patting thigh	Come to heel/range towards handler
Right arm outstretched	Range to right
Left arm outstretched	Range to left
Overhand push	Range away from handler

Not all those commands will be required by the shooting man who simply wants a retriever for wildfowling purposes, but dog training is an interesting and rewarding exercise in its own right and it is satisfying to take a dog beyond purely utilitarian stages.

By the time the puppy is about six months old he should be responsive enough to commence serious training. Detailed instruction is outwith the scope of this book but the following basic exercises will provide the foundation for more advanced work.

Early schooling for a labrador puppy.

Retrieving a dummy from water.

Sitting

To teach the dog to sit, place one hand under his chin and the other hand on his rump. Give the command 'hup' and press down on the pup's hindquarters so that the sitting position is adopted. Hold here while you give enthusiastic praise. When the dog consistently sits immediately in response to the word 'hup', the verbal command should be accompanied by a raised hand so that the visual signal assumes the same meaning as the spoken instruction. At a later date a single blast on the whistle will be used with the word and the hand signal so that ultimately the puppy will respond to any one of the sit commands — voice, whistle or hand signal.

To proceed one step further, the dog is told to sit and the handler walks away with the right hand held up while giving the verbal command 'stay'. This exercise must be repeated in gentle stages with the handler frequently returning to praise the dog if it does stay or taking it back to its original position if it moves. Gradually the distance from the handler at which the dog is expected to stay can be increased until the handler can walk right out of sight and then return to find that his pupil has not moved.

The whistle command to sit and stay — known as the stop whistle — is particularly useful once the dog has learned to obey it at a distance. The ability to stop the dog from a distance is essential for some of the more advanced training exercises such as directional control.

Basic Retrieving

Early retrieving is taught with the help of a light dummy, such as a rolled-up sock, and a great deal of patience. It is important to call in the puppy as soon as he has picked up the dummy and to take it from him very gently indeed. When the sock is delivered, be really profuse in your praise. If the pup is reluctant to deliver the dummy to hand, it helps to carry out the early exercises in a confined space so that he cannot run off with the dummy in his mouth. After a while it will be possible to leave the pupil in the stay position and throw a dummy some distance. If he moves when the dummy is thrown, stop him with the whistle and take him back to the original position. It may be necessary to restrain him for a little while in that position before commanding him to retrieve.

For more advanced retriever training, directional control, teaching the dog to mark fallen game, teaching to scent and ensuring rock steadiness, it will help to be equipped with several dummies of varying weights and compositions, together with a dummy launcher which uses .22 blank cartridges and will throw a plastic dummy up to 100 yards. A specialised book or a course of gundog training classes will provide the necessary information for teaching the pupil, and by the pup's first birthday he should be well on the way to becoming a real asset at flight time. Apart from earning his keep by retrieving shot wildfowl, a good gundog will be a fine companion and a joy to work.

A well-trained gundog will share its dinner with the hens.

11

Conservation and Research

Even before the organisation changed its name to the British Association for Shooting and Conservation, its predecessor, WAGBI, carried the subtitle 'For Shooting and Conservation' on its letterheads. One might expect that a conflict would exist between the ornithologist and the shotgunner, yet for several decades the positive link between sporting shooting and wildlife conservation has been emphasised by both groups. The essence of this partnership was encapsulated in a booklet, *The Story of a Triumvirate*, published jointly by the Nature Conservancy, the Wildfowlers' Association of Great Britain and Ireland and the Wildfowl Trust in 1970. As the late Sir Peter Scott, one of Britain's most eminent conservationists and founder of the Wildfowl Trust, wrote in the same year, 'As a natural resource,

Part of a conservation exhibition mounted by a wildfowling club.

wildfowl should be regarded as a legitimate crop and wildfowling is the traditional way of harvesting it. We must only be sure that the harvest is there to gather.'

Metaphorically, if not literally, the wildfowler is on firm ground when he claims to have made a meaningful contribution to wildlife conservation. From his position in the mud of an estuary or saltmarsh, he must fully understand the behaviour of duck and geese, as only after mastering every detail of their habits and habitat can he hope to outwit them at morning flight. Perhaps it is the intense communion between fowler and fowl which leads to an interest in conservation. Certainly wildfowlers cannot fail to notice the adverse effects of marshland drainage and coastal industry upon the populations of the birds they pursue.

At every level, from individual fowler to vast international organisations, there is a clear need for responsible shooting and effective conservation to be seen as compatible bedfellows. By talking in those terms we do not intend to suggest that sportsmen should adopt the 'sweet little dicky bird' mentality which views the world of nature through rose-coloured spectacles — rose-coloured spectacles which are often tinted to the point of opacity. When a sportsman-conservationist kills a goose, the bird is every bit as dead as a starling slain by an airgun-toting urban vandal. But when the wildfowler turns his hand to duck rearing or habitat improvement, he does it equally well.

In the vanishing landscape of the British countryside, it is the wetlands which have been eroded fastest. The twin pressures of agricultural development and industrial growth have eaten up vast tracts of marsh and fen which once provided an ideal environment for wildfowl. In other countries, also, prime duck and goose habitat has disappeared or been threatened in a similar manner. Later in this chapter consideration will be given to some of the national and international measures which have been taken to alleviate the situation, but first it would seem apposite to discuss a few of the means by which a local contribution might be made to the well-being of the quarry species.

Duck Rearing

One positive way in which the wildfowler can begin to re-sow some of his harvest is to rear a few duck each year and release them on to secluded waters. Of all birds, duck are amongst the easiest to care for and mallard is the ideal species for the novice.

Incubation
Eggs can be hatched either under broody hens or bantams, or in an artificial incubator heated by paraffin or electricity. The more modern models have electronic thermostatic controls but the older capsule type is still capable of giving reliable service on a small scale. Wildfowling clubs and shooting

Mallard eggs set in the incubator of a wildfowling club.

syndicates will certainly find that a small electronic incubator is a worthwhile investment, provided that the instructions are followed to the letter and that absolute cleanliness is maintained.

I shamefully remember my own first attempt at incubating eggs in an old ironclad still air machine. I took the temperature at the wrong height, eggs were never candled to check humidity and the equipment was not scrubbed and fumigated prior to use. The eggs of several species with different incubation periods were set together and, so confident was I, the incubator was packed with bantam eggs from a neighbour's hen run and precious ornamental pheasant eggs belonging to a friend, in addition to my mallard eggs. When only a few chicks hatched, the need for much greater care was firmly and embarrassingly driven home.

The up-to-date incubator pictured on page 137 is a very different proposition and with it my local wildfowling club annually hatches off at least ninety per cent of the mallard eggs which have been set. It is clean, easily maintained and virtually foolproof, and it looks so attractive that it is not unknown for a brood of ducklings to be hatched in a member's bedroom.

When incubating duck eggs, it is vital to ensure that the humidity is kept at the correct level and to turn the eggs several times each day. A handy tip in this regard is to mark each egg with a pencil cross and turn so that the crosses face up and down alternately. Try to turn the eggs through 180° at least three times in each twenty-four period until the twenty-fifth day. For the last three days they need not be turned but, instead, should be lightly sprayed twice-daily with a little warm water.

Brooding
When the eggs hatch the ducklings should be left in the incubator for about twelve hours to dry off and then transferred to a brooding pen. These little birds are so undemanding and trouble-free that they can be brooded in a wooden box under an ordinary domestic electric light bulb although, in reality, it is simple and inexpensive to build a proper pen and utilise an

It is a simple matter to erect a pen in which to rear a few duck.

infra-red heater of the dull-emitter type. The correct height for the lamp or heater is judged by observing the ducklings. If they huddle together under it, the bulb requires to be lowered; if they stay at the edges of the pen, it should be raised a little.

For the first three weeks it is prudent to provide heat for twenty-four hours each day, simply raising the heater a few inches at the end of each week. During week four it can be switched off for an increasing length of time on successive days until, by the end of that week, artificial heat may be dispensed with entirely and the ducklings moved to a larger pen out of doors.

Food and Water

Throughout this period the birds may be fed with standard chick crumbs to which have been added some chopped lettuce or other greens. At the end of their fourth week, poultry growers' pellets should be gradually substituted for the crumbs and this diet will suffice until the ducklings are ready for release.

Although, in the wild, young duck take to the water almost immediately after hatching, it must be remembered that hand-reared birds do not have a protective coating of oil from their mother to waterproof their down. It is

The first ducklings hatch.

important, therefore, that artificially brooded ducklings are not permitted to get wet until they are well feathered lest they chill and die. Accordingly, their water container should be arranged so that they can wet their bills thoroughly but cannot hop in for a bath. It is surprising how much water a few mallard ducklings get through. They splash it everywhere and delight in making a soggy mash with their crumbs.

When they are old enough to be put in a movable pen on the garden lawn, care should be taken to use wire mesh which is fine enough to exclude small birds; not because sparrows might steal the ducklings' food but rather to avoid trapped song birds being killed by the young duck. The best age at which to release the ducklings into the wild is probably at around eight weeks. To keep them in the garden for much longer would be likely to result in over-tameness and the risk that the birds would fail to survive in the wild. The release location should be chosen with care with an eye to calm water, shelter, freedom from predators and ample feeding.

It is advisable to resist the temptation to visit the young duck every few days. Whereas it is natural to wonder how they are coping in the wild, frequent contact with humans may prevent them developing the necessary level of caution which is so essential to survival in any wild species.

Habitat Improvement

The second way in which a group of fowlers can meaningfully contribute to wildfowl conservation is by adopting a small lake or pool and improving its

A wildfowler cleaning up his local marsh.

potential as a duck habitat. Virtually any area of water can be used, but barren flooded gravel pits in which workings have ended are a favourite on account of the dramatic transformation which can readily be effected.

First steps are to alter the landscape in such a way that the length of shoreline is maximised. Peninsulas and islands can be created, the latter being either built up from the bottom or floated on rafts of oil drums. Planting out must be done after systematic planning and the plants should be selected to provide both shelter and food. Marginal plants grow around the edges of the pool while emergent species are rooted below water but have aerial leaves. Floating and submerged plants will complete the list but there is no need to aim for a fantastic variety of vegetation. Those species which have naturally colonised other pools in the neighbourhood are the ones to consider first.

With a selection of reeds, rushes and sedges on the bank, a pondweed or crowfoot in the shallows and some duckweed on the surface, it is surprising how quickly a bare pit can become a green pond. Shrubs and trees planted a little distance back from the shoreline will not only add to the picture but will also provide shelter from strong winds.

Some really excellent work has been done by wildfowling clubs throughout the country and there have been a number of outstanding successes in converting old pit workings and similar areas of industrial dereliction into fine wildfowl sanctuaries. Of international fame in this respect is the splendid gravel pit experimental reserve at Sevenoaks which was masterminded by the late Dr Jeffery Harrison.

Nature Reserves

At a more official level, the conservation of wildfowl and wetland habitat has been a major consideration in the creation of all manner of nature reserves, sanctuaries and refuges. The Nature Conservancy Council has responsibility for advising the government on the control and conservation of all natural flora and fauna in Britain and for establishing, maintaining and managing nature reserves. National nature reserves such as those at Bridgwater Bay, Scolt Head Island, Lindisfarne, Caerlaverock and Loch Leven are attempts to preserve important wildfowl habitats for future generations. On some National Nature Reserves controlled shooting is allowed under a permit system.

Since 1952 there has been an increasing movement towards setting up local nature reserves and, in coastal areas, much of the pressure has come from wildfowling clubs which have recognised that control is essential if the well-being of the quarry species is to be assured. The bureaucracy of local government can grind exceedingly slowly and some fowling clubs have had to be very patient while their proposals gradually took shape. Despite such initial problems, success has been achieved in many areas and a number of local nature reserves feature the representation of wildfowling

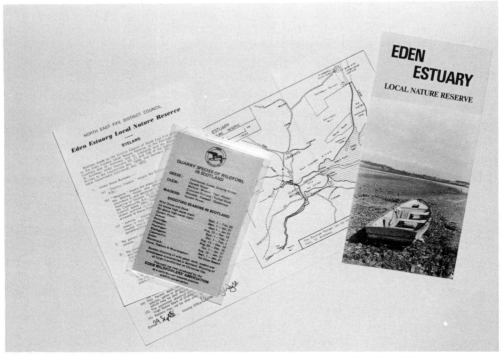

In some areas local nature reserves have been promoted by wildfowling clubs.

interests on their management committees. The selflessness of fowlers is evident also in the many thousands of acres of club-controlled land and foreshore which have been designated as sanctuary areas and upon which no shooting takes place.

Research

If may seem a paradox that wildfowlers — those hardy, self-sufficient gunners of the remote and windswept marshes — should be so ready to co-operate with modern, high-technology scientific research into the habits and habitat of their quarry and the ways in which their sport might impinge upon the natural order. Yet, over the years, a great deal of survey work has been undertaken by wildfowlers in order to give us a better understanding of the duck and geese and their natural environment. The British Association for Shooting and Conservation, long before it changed its title from WAGBI, has been at the forefront of this activity. The Association's headquarters at Marford Mill houses a dedicated team of trained scientists.

Duck Wing Survey

One of the early research projects undertaken by WAGBI — and continued by the BASC — was the Duck Wing survey. For over a decade, many fowlers have been carefully removing one wing from every duck which they shoot and, at the end of the season, have been sending them to the BASC. From an analysis of those duck wings it is possible not only to analyse the national wildfowling bag in terms of species but, more saliently, to arrive at firm conclusions about the breeding success of different species in different years, and about the sex distribution on the wintering grounds. From the duck wings can be obtained much information about the species, sex and age of the birds which have been shot.

When information from the Duck Wing survey is combined with other data from, for instance, the National Shooting Survey, then even more interesting conclusions can be drawn.

Although widely used in the USA, further research is required before steel shot is imposed in Britain.

Lead Shot Poisoning

Another example of wildfowlers co-operating with scientific research occurred when concern was first expressed about the effect which ingested lead shot might have upon wildfowl mortality rates. In America, there had already been legislation to ban lead shot for waterfowling in several states and it looked as if some European countries might follow suit. For a number of seasons wildfowlers from all over Britain carefully wrapped up the viscera of all the birds they shot and sent the gruesome little plastic bags to Greg Mudge at the Wildfowl Trust.

Major die-offs of duck and geese as a result of lead poisoning are rare in Britain, although a notable exception was the loss of up to 500 greylag geese at Loch Spynie in 1986. In that isolated case, a dramatic lowering of the loch's water level allowed the geese access to mud and sediment which had previously been out of their reach and which contained an accumulation of lead shot deposited over many decades.

More research will be required on this subject and it is important that a wildfowling perspective should continue to inform the scientists. At the end of the day it is unlikely that lead shot poisoning of wildfowl will be found to be a serious problem in this country but, as people who profess to care for their quarry, it is right and proper that fowlers should be involved in the studies. It is also right and proper to assume that wildfowlers will take any action which is found to be necessary in particular localities where unusual combinations of circumstances lead to a problem being demonstrated.

Disturbance

The BASC has also co-operated with the Wildfowl Trust on a Wildfowling Disturbance Survey to determine whether wildfowling actually causes a harmful level of disturbance to wildfowl and waders. Many fowlers have completed questionnaires and Peter Fox at the BASC headquarters has actively co-ordinated other aspects of this research. The purpose of all research is, of course, to increase our knowledge of the birds which we hunt, the habitat in which they live and the factors which affect their well-being. Wildfowlers have always led the entire shooting community in terms of practical conservation and it is fitting that they should also show the way in terms of research.

There is, understandably, some serious soul-searching before any research project can be agreed. Wildfowlers have come to realise that some opponents of sporting shooting are a rather ill-principled collection of extremists who do not have a particularly high regard for the truth. There is always a fear, therefore, that any research findings might be twisted by the bird protectionists and used against us. At the end of the day, however, truth might be our only ally. That being so, it is important that we have the maximum amount of hard data and reliable information at our fingertips to contradict the lies of those opposed to sporting shooting.

At the same time, the wildfowling community must be ready to alter its practices if, on any particular issue, research unequivocally demonstrates that any of our quarry species are in serious danger. Conditions in Britain are fundamentally different from those in the USA and it is most unlikely that objective research will ever show that lead shot from wildfowling is significantly affecting the overall populations of wildfowl species in this country. If there was such an indication, however, then it would be reasonable to expect fowlers to take steps to minimise the harm.

Similarly, research might show up other factors which could be acted upon to improve the habitat of our quarry or avoid doing harm to the birds themselves. Without prejudging any issues, it is just conceivable that the disturbance research project might show that in certain areas under certain conditions there is the risk of an element of detrimental disturbance from wildfowling activities. In such a case, it would again be reasonable to expect wildfowlers to seriously consider whether measures such as extended sanctuary zones or time restrictions on shooting might be responsible steps to take.

The vital issue in all of this discussion is that the very last thing which we want is the danger of other people doing the research and then proscribing what wildfowlers must or must not do. It is far healthier that the fowling community is itself involved in the various studies and that we interpret the results coolly and objectively. At the end of the day, good sound information and scientifically proven facts are necessary to protect our own interests and those of the fowl which we hunt.

Pollution and Industry

The problems facing wildfowl populations are many. Oil pollution is a constant hazard in coastal waters and the watchdog mechanisms which have been set up to detect and minimise spillages are not always effective. Sea duck are particularly vulnerable, the 'oil on troubled waters' syndrome ironically making the oil slicks appear attractive to the fowl. Industrial development is a major threat to many of the estuaries of Britain and in the breeding grounds, too, there is an ever-present danger of habitat erosion due to the needs of a growing and more demanding human population making inroads into prime nesting habitat.

A feature of the past decade, however, has been an increasing awareness of environmental issues on the part of both public and politicians. It may be that some of the traditional threats will decline, but vigilance is still required by wildfowlers and other conservationists.

Not so long ago, the main pinkfooted goose breeding area on the vegetated oasis of Thjorsarver in central Iceland was threatened with flooding to create a massive reservoir for the purpose of providing hydro-electric power. The proposal to build an airport on the Maplin Sands would deprive dark-bellied brent geese of a major feeding area. The creation of polders in the Netherlands had dried out much prime marshland which was previously wildfowl habitat.

It is to compensate for these trends that international wildfowl conservation has become an increasingly vital concomitant of sporting shooting. In an age which has been characterised by the incessant march of concrete and steel, the man or woman who values the countryside and its wildlife must be prepared to work hard for its preservation.

12
From Gamebag to Table

In this age of mass-produced, plastic-wrapped, broiler chickens, the wildfowler has a unique opportunity to supply his family and friends with duck and geese which will really taste as fowl should. Whether a simple dish or a gourmet meal is desired, the flavour of well selected, carefully prepared and correctly cooked wildfowl is unbeatable. In general terms the palatability of duck and geese is affected by the diet of the birds. Those which have been feeding on grass or grain will have better-tasting flesh than others which have been subsisting upon a diet of molluscs or seaweed. Amongst the duck, surface feeders are normally a better bet than divers and both duck and geese, of whatever species, tend to be at their best early in the season.

A plump greylag goose makes a very fine meal.

The care which will ultimately reflect in the table-worthiness of the bird begins the moment it is shot. Wash all mud and ooze from the plumage and carefully fold the wings and neck before placing it in the bag. In this respect, a muslin or coarse canvas sack is better than a normal gamebag and, at all costs, plastic bags or waterproof-lined containers should be avoided. The fact that the fowl is well and truly dead does not mean that it no longer requires air. The more that can circulate around the feathers the better. Similarly, dead fowl should not be left in the boot of a car for longer than is absolutely necessary.

Hanging

Some writers have advocated hanging wildfowl to impart a gamey flavour but, personally, I prefer to hang the birds for only long enough to ensure that the flesh is tender. Young duck or geese can be prepared for the oven without any delay but older fowl may be the better for being hung for between three days and a fortnight depending upon their condition and the prevailing weather conditions. In mild temperatures a shorter period is necessary than in mid-winter. A bird which has been gut-shot should not be hung unless the viscera are first removed but, in normal circumstances, wildfowl should be hung before they are plucked and drawn.

Plucking

Traditionally, birds are plucked and the down is then removed by singeing. This operation is best undertaken out of doors and it helps to prevent feathers from being blown everywhere if the bird is held inside a paper sack or plastic bin-liner. Duck is easier to pluck than goose but care must be taken not to rip the skin. Pulling out the feathers a few at a time will prevent this happening. I must admit to a tendency to skin geese rather than pluck them and, although this is frowned upon by purists, it makes the job considerably quicker and the resultant loss of subcutaneous fat can be made good by placing a few rashers of streaky bacon over the carcass when roasting it.

An American idea which simplifies the plucking of duck is to remove all the large feathers and then cover the bird with molten paraffin wax, either by simply brushing it on or by dipping the whole carcass into a bucket of hot water on top of which the molten wax is floating. After the wax has cooled, it can be peeled off and, with luck, all the down and pin feathers will be cleanly removed. One word of caution — much of the wax which is sold in this country is produced for the purpose of making ornamental candles. If you buy a batch which contains incense, it might give the duck a rather unusual flavour!

Drawing

After plucking, the head, neck and lower legs should be cut off and the skin and muscle cut from vent to lower breastbone. The heart, lungs, windpipe, kidneys, liver and intestine are then removed and, if the bird is to be frozen, it should be wiped inside and out with a clean damp cloth. Alternatively, if the fowl is for immediate consumption, there is no harm in simply rinsing it under the cold tap. When freezing duck or geese, any sharp bones at the leg or wing should be taped before the bird is placed in a heavy gauge polythene bag. Remember to label the package adequately showing species, approximate age of bird and date of freezing.

A somewhat wasteful alternative to plucking and drawing wildfowl is to cut out the breast fillets. To do this, pluck only a row of feathers along the ridge of the breastbone. With a sharp knife, cut the skin and separate the subcutaneous fatty tissue from the meat. By cutting down the breastbone and around the rib cage, two prime fillets can be removed from each bird. I hate to see large duck treated in this manner as they contain so much more tender meat. There is little doubt, however, that the method is suitable for small birds such as teal or snipe and it is, of course, a standard procedure amongst woodpigeon shooters.

Recipes

There are many excellent methods of preparing and cooking wildfowl, using both conventional methods and the modern microwave oven. The following selection of recipes will provide the reader with an insight into the wide variety of dishes which use as a base the birds that he will bring back from a trip to the estuary.

Roast Wildfowl

The basic traditional method of cooking a duck or goose is to roast it. Normally wildfowl are served underdone to avoid drying out the flesh but those who prefer their fowl well roasted can overcome the problem by covering the breast with fatty bacon or basting the meat with wine or butter or both.

Pre-heat the oven to 425°F (220°C) or Gas mark 7 and put the birds, breast down, in a roasting tin. Baste with butter or wrap in foil. Allow forty-five to sixty minutes for a duck or twenty to twenty-five minutes per pound for a goose. Test for readiness by piercing a leg with a skewer — no juice should flow from a well-cooked bird but some clear liquid will be released by an underdone fowl.

Salmi of Wild Duck

	Sauce:
2 duck	500ml (1 pint) duck stock
3 medium carrots, sliced	50g (2oz) butter
3 medium onions, chopped	40g (1½oz) plain flour
6 rashers streaky bacon	125ml (¼ pint) red wine
1 orange, sectioned	salt and pepper
1 bay leaf	a few grapes, peeled and pipped

Make the stock using giblets, one carrot and one onion. Meanwhile cover duck breasts with bacon and put in a roasting tin with the remaining carrots and onions. Roast in a pre-heated oven set at 400°F (200°C) or Gas mark 6 for twenty-five to thirty minutes.

Lift the fowl out and slice meat from carcass. Strain the fat from the roasting tin and add 500ml (1 pint) duck stock. Heat until boiling then simmer to reduce liquid by one-third.

Make a roux by melting butter in a saucepan, add flour and cook until nutty brown. Remove from heat and stir in the reduced duck stock. Return pan to heat and boil for ½ minute, stirring continuously. Add red wine, salt and pepper to taste, and grapes. Pour over duck and cover with a lid or foil. Cook for thirty to thirty-five minutes in a pre-heated oven set to 350°F (180°C) or Gas mark 4.

Tenderising an Older Fowl
1 tired goose or duck
750ml (1½ pints) water
1 tablespoon lemon juice
1 bay leaf
1 onion, peeled and halved
2 level teaspoons salt

Stuff the bird if desired, truss and put it on the rack in a pressure cooker. Add water and other ingredients, fix lid and bring to pressure, allowing it to cook for thirty minutes.

While the fowl is being tenderised, set the oven at 350°F (180°C) or Gas mark 4. Ten minutes before the end of the pressure cooking time, put a roasting tin with fat into the oven.

After pressure cooking, reduce the pressure, lift lid, remove the bird and drain it well before placing it in the roasting tin. Roast in the usual way, basting twice during cooking. The stock which remains will make a first-class soup base.

Duck or goose treated in this way are delicious served with vegetables or, alternatively, they can be used in the following two recipes, both of which are useful methods of using up birds of indeterminate species or age which may be found at the bottom of the freezer just prior to the start of a new season.

Fowler's Pie
1 tenderised goose or two tenderised duck (see previous recipe)
50g (2oz) butter
1 large onion, peeled and chopped
40g (1½oz) plain flour
250ml (½ pint) wildfowl stock
salt and pepper
150g (5oz) mushrooms, sliced

200g (8oz) frozen puff pastry, thawed
1 egg, beaten

Remove the meat from goose or duck and cut into large chunks. Melt the butter in a saucepan, add meat and onion and fry until lightly browned. Add the flour and continue cooking for one minute, stirring continuously. Add the stock, bring to the boil, stirring well and skim if necessary. Season to taste, add mushrooms and turn into a pie dish.

Roll out pastry and cover pie dish. Make an airhole, decorate with pastry trimmings, brush with beaten egg and bake for forty minutes in a pre-heated oven set at 425°F (220°C) or Gas mark 7.

Wildfowl Pâté

150g (6oz) butter
1 goose liver or 2 duck livers
2 shallots, peeled and chopped
400g (1lb) cooked goose or duck meat, shredded
Grated rind and juice of 1 orange
4 tablespoons port or dry sherry
1 pinch dried rosemary
salt and pepper

Melt 25g (1oz) of the butter in a saucepan, add the liver and fry quickly until lightly browned on both sides. Remove and cool. Melt a further 25g (1oz) butter in the pan and add the shallots. Cook gently until soft but not brown.

Put the liver, duck or goose meat, shallots and 75g (3oz) of the remaining butter through the fine blade of a mincer twice and mix well together. Add the orange rind and juice, port or sherry, rosemary, salt and pepper. Put into a dish and seal with the remaining butter, melted. Leave overnight in a refrigerator.

Goose Mousse

1 x 70g (2½oz) packet aspic jelly powder
500ml (1 pint) goose stock
400g (1lb) cooked goose meat, shredded
100m (4 fl oz) dry sherry
1 teaspoon dried tarragon pepper
1 tablespoon tomato puree
250ml (½ pint) double cream

Make up the aspic jelly using the stock, following the instructions on the packet. Leave to cool and, when on the point of setting, put it into a liquidiser with the goose meat, sherry, tarragon and pepper. Blend until smooth and then beat in the cream and tomato puree. Turn into a wetted mould, 1½ litre (2 pint) size. Place in a refrigerator and leave until set. Turn out to serve.

Microwave Cookery

A microwave oven can revolutionise the cooking of wildfowl. Dishes can be prepared in a fraction of the usual time by microwaving to cook fresh food, thaw frozen birds or re-heat previously prepared dishes.

Points to Remember

Timing is crucially important when cooking by microwave as a few extra seconds can result in over-cooked food. It is better to cook for the minimum time suggested, then test the goose or duck meat for readiness. Cook for longer if required. Microwaved duck or goose is ready to serve when the inside is slightly pink and the juices run clear.

If your microwave cooker does not brown food, you can brown pieces of duck or goose in a frying pan first or microwave whole birds in a roasting bag. Alternatively, brush the skin with a mixture of soy sauce and melted butter before cooking. Completed dishes can be browned under the grill for a few minutes to give a crisper appearance if desired.

Many existing wildfowl recipes can be adapted for microwave cooking by referring to the instruction book for your specific appliance. The following two recipes have been specially compiled for the microwave and are truly delicious. They are based on 650 power microwave ovens.

St Clement's Duck

4 duck breast fillets, or
750g (1½lb) duck meat trimmed off bone
lemon and orange segments to garnish

Marinade:

2 tablespoons oil
juice of ½ lemon
½ teaspoon nutmeg
1 tablespoon chopped mixed herbs

Sauce:

½ orange, segmented
½ teaspoon cornflour
1 tablespoon water
salt and pepper

Mix marinade in a shallow dish, add the duck and coat well. Cover and marinate for four hours or overnight in a refrigerator, turning the meat occasionally. Drain and keep the marinade.

Place butter in a large dish and melt it. Add drained duck, cover and cook for five minutes at High setting (100%). Stir meat and then pour marinade over duck and cook at Medium setting (50%) for a further 5 minutes or until duck is tender. Taste and add salt and pepper as required.

Mix cornflour and water. Add to duck, stirring well. Cook at High (100%) for three minutes, stirring every minute. Add segmented orange and stir well. Garnish with lemon and orange segments before serving.

Wildfowl Casserole

900g (2lb) goose or duck pieces on the bone
25g (1oz) butter
2 tablespoons cornflour
3 tablespoons honey
1 tablespoon soy sauce
100g (4oz) sliced mushrooms
150g (6oz) mixed frozen vegetables

Marinade:

2 tablespoons oil
4 tablespoons cider vinegar, lemon juice or wine
1 small onion, finely chopped
1 clove garlic, crushed
150ml (¼ pint) cider or wine
salt and pepper

Mix marinade ingredients in a shallow dish. Add the goose or duck pieces. Cover and marinade for six to eight hours, turning occasionally to allow the flavours to enhance the meat. Drain the meat and reserve the marinade.

Melt butter in a large dish. Beat in the cornflour and gradually add the marinade, honey and soy sauce. Cook at High setting (100%) for three to four minutes until thickened, stirring two or three times.

Add the meat, stir well, cover and cook at Medium (50%) for thirty to thirty-five minutes or until tender.

Add the vegetables and cook for a further five minutes. Allow casserole to stand for ten minutes before serving.

Stuffings

There are many stuffings which can be used to retain the shape and aid the flavour of roast wildfowl. The traditional sage and onion is excellent but my family prefers fruity stuffings with duck or geese. This orange, apple and prune version is a firm favourite:

100g (4oz) prunes, stewed and stoned
1 orange, peel grated finely and fruit segmented
200g (8oz) cooking apples, peeled and cored
100g (4oz) rice, cooked
50g (2oz) shredded suet
salt and pepper
1 egg, beaten

Cut the prunes into quarters, roughly chop the apples and mix all the ingredients together. Bind with a beaten egg.

13
Close Season Pursuits

Although the coastal gunner may only shoot geese and duck between 1 September and the following 20 February, a keen wildfowler need not lose touch with his sport during the remainder of the year. Indeed, finding sufficient days to follow all of the activities which might be considered ancillary to the pursuit of fowl can present something of a problem to the man who must also devote time to the mundane task of earning a living.

The topics of duck rearing, habitat improvement and gundog training have already been considered and all three can occupy much of the fowler's attention during the close season. The sportsman who belongs to a wildfowling club will probably find that there is a variety of events organised during the spring and summer; clay pigeon shooting and gundog working tests being two which readily spring to mind as activities which may possibly become consuming interests in their own right.

Above all else, the warmer days of the year provide opportunities for getting to know the marsh, the surrounding countryside and the wildlife which inhabits the area. Whether one is out with gun, camera, binoculars or merely an open set of eyes and ears, there is much to be observed which will be of benefit when the wildfowling season arrives once more.

Vermin Control

One excellent way of maintaining a shooting interest throughout the summer is to seek to undertake vermin control for a few local farmers. Almost all agricultural enterprises suffer from the attentions of rabbits or woodpigeons and shooting either or both can provide a worthwhile service to the farm and sport for the shooter.

Do not expect, however, to be welcomed with open arms at every farmhouse which you approach. Others may have been there before and not all have paid proper respect to the crops, stock, fences and gates. Indeed, convincing the farmer that you are a responsible person with an adequate knowledge of the countryside and its ways may be a difficult task. Style of approach is important and obtaining permission to shoot is always easier if you dress respectably and conduct yourself politely. It is amazing the difference that a clean shirt and a tie can make on these occasions. Stress that you will always be alone and that you will always consult before commencing shooting so that the owner's wishes might be observed at all times. Above all, do not permit yourself the arrogance of assuming that you are doing the farmer a favour by killing his vermin. There are a dozen local Guns who would gladly do the same. Rather, regard yourself as being the principal benefactor of the arrangement as you will enjoy as much sport from a fruitful day in a pigeon hide as many who have paid out hundreds of pounds for the privilege of a few hours on a covert shoot.

Clay Pigeon Shooting

The other method of obtaining shotgun practice throughout the close season is to participate in a little clay pigeon shooting. There is not space here to deal in detail with the intricacies of every discipline which may be

Clay pigeon practice can help to rectify shooting faults.

followed by a clay-shooting enthusiast but the main types are known as skeet, down-the-line and sporting. The latter possibly provides the most interest for the casual Shot as the 'birds' are presented in a variety of ways, both singly and as pairs. The various stands bear names which indicate the type of natural quarry which the clay is intended to simulate, for example springing teal, high pheasant, driven partridge and so forth.

The little black saucers of plaster and pitch are sprung from a mechnical trap at a call from the shooter and scoring can be very high indeed in top class competitions, frequently the single target dropped out of one hundred being the decider. At that level clay-shooting can become a very addictive sport and, on account of the number of cartridges used, it is also extremely expensive.

Practice

Given that the wildfowler is likely to be concerned with obtaining practice outwith the fowling season, he might be well advised to avoid the serious competitive events and attend some of the smaller clay shoots. There are many specialist clay clubs throughout the country and most wildfowling and roughshooting associations also run informal clay pigeon events. The atmosphere at the latter is generally more relaxed and this makes them a better bet for the novice who does not aspire to becoming an Olympic competitor. Many country fairs also feature sporting clay shoots and these can be great fun if they are not taken too seriously.

Even more useful is a small trap bought jointly by three or four friends which can be taken out and used for practice on a warm summer evening. In this way each Gun can repeat and study the types of shot which give him trouble. Flighting geese and duck can be simulated and matters of lead, swing and timing perfected. It should be borne in mind, however, that a clay pigeon is decelerating from the moment it leaves the trap while, on the other hand, the wildfowler's natural quarry is usually accelerating or travelling at fairly uniform velocity. In addition, a clay pigeon cannot suddenly alter course and swerve or jink when it sees the fowler! For those reasons, clay shooting can never exactly replicate the shots which the wildfowler will encounter on the marsh. Having said that, the differences are not so great as to negate the value of clay practice.

Home Loading

A wildfowler has been described as one who goes out light hearted and returns empty handed. The man who restricts his shooting to the saltmarsh beteween the months of September and February is consequently unlikely to work his way through many boxes of cartridges in the course of a season. If, however, vermin control and clay pigeon shooting are practised with any great frequency, the gun's appetite for ammunition might become positively voracious and the cartridges to feed it will be a significant drain on the pocket. In these circumstances some thought might be given to reloading spent cartridge cases with new primers, powder, wads and shot.

Home loading is a profitable way of spending the odd evening and the money to be saved can be fairly substantial if many cartridges are used each year. At one time it was normal to refer to the two methods of reloading — by hand tools and by machine — but very inexpensive plastic machines have become available in recent years and if it is worth reloading cartridges at all, it is certainly worth investing in one of those. They are virtually fool-proof and the chance of a dangerous error occurring is reduced to a minimum.

Stages in Reloading

In essence, the process of reloading a shotgun cartridge can be broken down into a simple sequence of operations:

1. Decapping.
2. Resizing the case and head.
3. Recapping with a fresh primer.
4. Filling with a measured quantity of powder.
5. Inserting and ramming the wads.
6. Filling with the correct weight of lead shot.
7. Closing the end of the cartridge case.

According to the type of machine used, some of these operations may be combined. A point worth watching when choosing equipment is that some models are suitable only for a certain brand of primer or wad and others can produce only a single style of closure. The best machines can utilise different primers, will load either felt or plastic wads and have interchange-able crimp dies. At the highest level of sophistication, fully automatic equipment is available which passes each case round several stations and produces one reloaded cartridge at each stroke of the handle. With simpler types of machine it is no bad idea to standardise on components and some thought should be given to the alternatives before choosing a particular model.

Standardisation

Most British factory loaded cartridges have plastic cases and are closed by means of a six-segment crimp. If large quantities of empties are picked up after a major clay pigeon shoot it will be noticed that some foreign brands differ in case design and have an eight-point crimp closure. Discard any which do not conform to your standard type or which are split or damaged in any way.

Either felt or plastic wads may be used and, once more, it is worthwhile standardising on one brand and using nothing else. Despite the temptation, do not re-use old plastic wads which have been picked up at a clay pigeon ground. Because case lengths, powder densities and wad types change fairly frequently, I will not give any 'recipes' here. Rather the fowler is advised to procure current copies of the loading tables which are published by many of the component manufacturers or, alternatively, to use the tables which appear as regular items in several of the popular shooting periodicals. These should be up-to-date in terms of the components which are specified.

The quantities given must be followed precisely as, with modern materials, the slightest excess of either powder or shot can produce dangerous combustion pressures. The same danger arises if an unsuitable primer/powder combination is used or the wrong type of case employed.

Economy

As the price of lead shot fluctuates, so too does the financial benefit to be gained from home loading. On average, the standard reloaded 12-gauge game or clay cartridge should show a saving of about 20% on the cost of factory produced ammunition but the magnum user may find his outlay reduced by up to 50% and the big-bore enthusiast, although he may have to use hand tools, will be delighted to discover that his reloads cost only a quarter of the price of the commercial product. Really keen home loaders can make the enterprise even more rewarding by pouring their own shot from scrap lead.

Country Fairs

An annual event which is worth a visit when it comes within travelling distance is the Game Fair organised by the Country Landowners' Association. Each year this is a massive jamboree of interest to anyone who participates in field sports. On a smaller scale, there is an increasing number of country fairs organised by local groups of sportsmen and these can be fun to visit or to help organise. Clay pigeon shooting, gundog tests and scurries, pigeon plucking contests, terrier racing and angling competitions are only a few of the attractions on such occasions. There will also be many trade stands where the fowler can examine the latest in guns, clothing and accessories.

Public Relations

The sportsman who assists at his local fair — whether it be as a car park marshal, keeping scores at the clays or assisting on a club stand or in the BASC shop — will make a host of new friends and learn a lot about other country sports. Not a matter of small importance, a successful fair can raise substantial funds which may then be put to good use in promoting field sports. As an example, in my own part of the country, the annual Tayside Field Sports Fair has now resulted in many thousands of pounds being applied to worthy causes, including the promotion and defence of wildfowling.

Helping at a country fair is a pleasant way of spending a few days in summer.

The educative aspects of inviting the general public to spend a day amongst country sportsmen should not be overlooked either. A happy Saturday in the countryside is a fine introduction to the world of shooting and fishing for many youngsters from nearby conurbations. For the sake of the future of our sport, all wildfowlers should play their part in public relations activities of this sort.

Photography

As mentioned in an earlier chapter, one of the most effective ways of 'practising' wildfowling during the close season is to substitute a camera for the shotgun and go out shooting with film rather than lead pellets. Inexpensive equipment is perfectly adequate, the cheapest 35mm reflex camera augmented by the least costly 400mm telephoto lens and a rifle grip being capable of producing perfectly acceptable results. With inexpensive equipment there is not the attendant worry of getting it damaged by spatterings of foreshore mud — a fear which would greatly concern the owner of an expensive sophisticated outfit.

A Selective Approach

There are a number of different approaches to this pastime, one being to capture on celluloid as many different species of wildfowl as possible in much the same manner as the great hunter-naturalists of the past collected corpses. More satisfying is to undertake a systematic study attempting, for instance, to photograph the different plumage phases of a single species or to obtain photographs of the birds of a small selected habitat.

Whichever way the subject is tackled, stalking fowl with a camera in daylight will release to the wildfowler a great deal of knowledge which will be of direct assistance to him when the shooting season comes round again. Exactly the same principles of concealment and camouflage apply when one is aiming through a viewfinder as when the quarry is sighted over the barrels of a shotgun. It is a tragedy that so many shore-shooters hope to become familiar with both the topography of the saltings and the habits of their quarry merely by going out for a couple of dozen dawn flights each year. That many give up the sport after a few fruitless seasons is not too surprising.

Conclusion

There then, in a few short pages, is a taste of some of the ways in which the wildfowler might while away the months between February and September. The fowling season occupies less than half the year but one need never be far away from the estuary in either body or spirit. With the spring and summer having been profitably spent, the anticipation of wild birds in wild places on wild mornings will be all the greater.

APPENDIX A

Selected Bibliography

The literature of wildfowling and wildfowl is particularly extensive and simply to provide a lengthy catalogue of titles would be of little value to the average reader. The following summary of suggested further reading has been selected by the author to provide a balanced bookshelf for novice and veteran alike. Anyone wishing to make an academic study of wildfowling literature should use the extensive bibliography contained in *The New Wildfowler (3rd Edition)* as a starting point.

Wildfowling Past and Present

Payne-Gallwey, Sir R., *The Fowler in Ireland*, 1882

Millais, J. G., *The Wildfowler in Scotland*, 1901

Duncan, S. and Thorne, G., *The Complete Wildfowler*, 1911

Parker, E. (Ed), *Col Hawker's Shooting Diaries*, 1931

Scott, P., *Morning Flight*, 1935

Cadman, A., *Tales of a Wildfowler*, 1957

Willock, C., *Kenzie the Wild Goose Man*, 1972

Humphreys, J., *Stanley Duncan – Wildfowler*, 1983

Begbie, E., *Fowler in the Wild*, 1987

Swan, M., *Fowling for Duck*, 1988

Jarrett, A., *One Winter's Tale*, 1988

Begbie, E. (Ed), *The New Wildfowler (3rd Edition)*, 1989

Natural History of Wildfowl

Ogilvie, M. A., *Ducks of Britain and Europe*, 1976

Ogilvie, M. A. *Wild Geese*, 1978

Owen, M. *Wildfowl of Europe*, 1977

Martin, B. P., *Sporting Birds of the British Isles*, 1984

Madge, S. and Burn, H., *Wildfowl*, 1988

Miscellaneous

Burrard, Major Sir G., *The Modern Shotgun (3 volumes)*, 1931

Thomas, G., *Shotguns and Cartridges for Game and Clays*, 1975

Moxon, P. R. A., *Training the Roughshooter's Dog*, 1977

Begbie, E., *The Sportsman's Companion*, 1981

McDougall, D., *8-Bore Ammunition*, 1985

Humphreys, J., *Hunter's Fen*, 1986

Parkes, C. and Thornley, J., *Fair Game*, 1987

Skinner, J., *Through the Lens with Stanley Duncan*, 1988

APPENDIX B

Useful Addresses

British Association for Shooting and Conservation

Headquarters:
Marford Mill, Rossett, Clwyd, LL12 0HL.

Regional Offices:
South and West England: Smokey Bottom Lodge, Staple Fitzpaine, Taunton, Somerset, TA3 5BL.

East and South-East England: King's Forest Office, West Stow, Bury St Edmunds, Suffolk, IP28 6HA.

Wales and West Midlands: Marford Mill, Rossett, Clwyd, LL12 0HL.

Northern England: 2 Old Stable Courtyard, Broughton, Skipton, North Yorkshire, BD23 3AE.

Northern Ireland: The Courtyard Cottage, Calgorm Castle, Ballymena, Co Antrim, BT42 8HL.

Scotland: Croft Cottage, Trochry, By Dunkeld, Perthshire, PH8 0DY.

Game Conservancy, Fordingbridge, Hampshire.

Wildfowl Trust, The New Grounds, Slimbridge, Gloucestershire.

British Field Sports Society, 59 Kennington Road, London, SE1 7PZ.

Royal Society for the Protection of Birds, The Lodge, Sandy, Bedfordshire.

Clay Pigeon Shooting Association, 107 Epping New Road, Buckhurst Hill, Essex, IG9 5TQ.

Kennel Club, 1-4 Clarges Street, Piccadilly, London, W1Y 8AB.

Birmingham Gun Barrel Proof House, Banbury Street, Birmingham, B5 5RH.

London Proof House, The Gunmakers Company, 48 Commercial Road, London, E1L 1LP.

APPENDIX C

Data Tables

A comprehensive tabulation of ballistic data may be found in *The Shooter's Diary*, which is published annually by **Eley Ltd.**

Table 1   Nominal diameter of bore

Bore Number	8-bore	10-bore	12-bore	16-bore	20-bore	28-bore
Diameter (inches)	.835	.775	.729	.662	.615	.550

Table 2   Shot sizes

Shot Size	Nominal Diameter (inches)	No. of Pellets per oz
AAA	.20	35
BB	.16	70
1	.14	100
3	.12	140
4	.11	170
5	.105	220
6	.10	270
7	.095	340

Table 3   Approximate shot size equivalents

British	French	Italian	American
BB	1	00	Air Rifle
1	3	2	2
3	4	3	4
4	5	4	5
5	6	5	6
6	—	6	—
7	7	7	7½

Table 4   Percentage of pellets falling in 30″ circle at various ranges

Choke Boring	Range (yards)				
	20	30	40	50	60
True cylinder	80%	60%	40%	27%	17%
Imp. cyl.	92%	72%	50%	33%	22%
¼-choke	100%	77%	55%	38%	25%
½-choke	100%	83%	60%	41%	27%
¾-choke	100%	92%	65%	46%	30%
Full choke	100%	100%	70%	50%	33%

APPENDIX D

Proof Marks

As mentioned in Chapter 6, the *Proof Acts* lay down that no small arm may be sold, exchanged or exported, exposed or kept for sale or exchange or pawned unless and until it has been fully proved and duly marked.

Guns proved in Britain for smokeless or nitro powders will bear one of the following marks on the barrels:

     And/or the words NITRO PROOF

Guns proved in Britain prior to 1904 may bear the following proof marks which invariably indicate proof for black powder only unless they are associated with the marking Nitro Proof in words:

It is vital that a gun proved for use with black powder is not used with modern cartridges. In view of the age of such a gun, it would be prudent to submit it for reproof in any case.

The proof marks of the following foreign countries are currently acceptable in Britain:

Austria (Ferlach and Vienna)	West Germany
Belgium	Italy
Czechoslovakia	Republic of Ireland
France (Paris and St Etienne)	Spain

Further details of proof requirements and markings are contained in the booklet *Notes on the Proof of Shotguns and other Small Arms* issued under the joint authority of the London and Birmingham proof authorities.

In any case of doubt a competent gunmaker should be consulted.

Index